Parents and Teachers Working Together

Parents and Teachers Working Together

Addressing School's Most Vital Stakeholders

Brett J. Novick

ROWMAN & LITTLEFIELD
Lanham • Boulder • New York • London

Published by Rowman & Littlefield
A wholly owned subsidiary of The Rowman & Littlefield Publishing Group, Inc.
4501 Forbes Boulevard, Suite 200, Lanham, Maryland 20706
www.rowman.com

Unit A, Whitacre Mews, 26-34 Stannary Street, London SE11 4AB

British Library Cataloguing in Publication Information Available

Library of Congress Cataloging-in-Publication Data
Names: Novick, Brett J.
Title: Parents and teachers working together addressing school's most vital
   stakeholders / Brett J. Novick.
Description: Lanham, Maryland : Rowman & Littlefield, 2016. |
   Includes bibliographical references and index.
Identifiers: LCCN 2016042610 (print) | LCCN 2016043101 (ebook) |
   ISBN 9781475828870 (cloth : alk. paper) | ISBN 9781475828887 (pbk. : alk. paper) |
   ISBN 9781475828894 (Electronic)
Subjects: LCSH: Parent-teacher relationships. | Conflict management.
Classification: LCC LC226 .N68 2016 (print) | LCC LC226 (ebook) |
   DDC 371.19/2—dc23
LC record available at https://lccn.loc.gov/2016042610

♾ ™ The paper used in this publication meets the minimum requirements of American National Standard for Information Sciences—Permanence of Paper for Printed Library Materials, ANSI/NISO Z39.48-1992.

Printed in the United States of America

I would like to dedicate this book to my late father Dr. William Novick, who taught me how to be a father. To my parents who taught me the importance of hard work and values. My wife Darla, who teaches me each and every day how to be a better person, parent, and spouse. My children Billy, and Samantha, who give me hope for a future generation with pride. Also, to the many students, parents, and educators that I have had the honor of working with over the years, who have taught me so very much. Please know it was an honor for me to be allowed to play a small part in your lives. The many mentors who, in both education and life, inspired me in every aspect. Finally, a heartfelt thank you to the publishers and staff at Rowman & Littlefield for your confidence in publishing this book and to you, the reader, for taking precious time out of your schedule to read my book. Thank you.

Contents

Foreword

We expect teachers to handle teenage pregnancy, substance abuse, and the failings of the family. Then we expect them to educate our children.

—John Sculley*

The above comment, made by John Sculley while CEO of Apple Computer, Inc., has been widely quoted by education advocates and professionals for over 20 years. And, it has never been more true to life than it is today. Children and teenagers get conflicted messages from peers, media, and family, and while "family values" may still be a popular phrase, the meaning thereof is becoming increasingly blurred. Children and teens are still generally told by their parents and teachers to avoid "bad influences" (drugs, sex, etc.), but these messages are becoming drowned in the sea of social media, which is often filled with provocative images, bullying, and a general sense of self-centeredness.

Developmentally, as children become teens, they gradually shift focus toward fitting in with peers, and grow more susceptible to peer influence. This influence seems to now come from all over—not just from Facebook and Instagram pages, but also from tweets, YouTube videos, and messages exchanged through a plethora of texting apps teens use nowadays to hide their communications from their parents. The shift away from family and toward peers appears to occur earlier and earlier. It is not unusual for parents to report that their 10-year-olds now are much more influenced by their peers, and are exposed to much more mature content than their 18-year-olds were when they were this age just 8 years ago. In sum, parents feel they are increasingly losing control over the influences that shape their children. This loss of control is accompanied by frustration, anger, and often desperation to arrest or reverse some of these factors.

Indeed, parents have legitimate reasons to worry. Nearly half of high school students become sexually active, and 41% don't use condoms (CDC, 2013). About half of all sexually transmitted diseases occur in teenagers and college-age adults, and in 2013, 10,000 cases of AIDS were diagnosed in individuals under age of 25 (CDC).

While rates of teenage pregnancy in the United States are dropping, the US teen birth rate is still much higher than many other developed countries, including Canada (US Department of Health & Human Services, 2014). The same report acknowledges that birth rates among teens are more than twice as likely among Latino teens (38 per 1000) and African American teens (34.9 per 1000) than their Caucasian counterparts (17 per 1000). About 89% of these births occur outside of marriage, and about 77% of these pregnancies are unplanned. Clearly, a significant portion of teenagers become sexually active at a young age, and they tend to do so with limited responsibility, facts that trouble many parents and undoubtedly cause them many sleepless nights.

Even more alarming is the exposure of teenagers to alcohol and drugs of abuse. In 2014, 9% of 8th graders, 23.5% of 10th graders, and 37.4% of 12th graders admitted to past-month use of alcohol, and nearly 20% admitted to binge drinking in the previous 2 weeks (National Institute on Drug Abuse, 2014).

Marijuana use was reported by 12% of 8th graders and over one-third of high school seniors. Over 80% of high school students and over one-third of middle school students reported that marijuana is easy to obtain. About 44% of school students knew a student selling drugs at their high school, and 75% of 12- to-17-year-olds reported that seeing pictures of peers "partying" (with alcohol or drugs) on social media encouraged them to do the same (National Center on Addiction and Substance Abuse, 2012).

While heroin use among teens has leveled off, such use is now common in suburban neighborhoods, and 29.7% of 12th graders and 12.6% of 8th graders say that they can obtain heroin (CDC, 2014). The death rate due to drug overdose among teenagers and young adults has doubled in the past decade, reaching 7.3 per 100,000 in 2011–2013 (Trust for America's Health, 2015). Thus, parents have a solid basis for their worries.

With so many negative influences all around, parents look for sources of positive influence in their children's lives. Naturally, schools come to mind, as children gradually start to spend more time in school than they spend awake at home. Indeed, education is a powerful force that can change people's lives. Those with high school education live longer, healthier, and earn more money than those who drop out, and, generally speaking, the higher the education the higher the standard of living. So, parents hope that good education will improve their children's prospects for the future.

Schools also provide other positive influences. Classes in art, music, science, etc. expose students to directions in life that may spark their curiosity, pique their interest, and spur growth and further educational pursuits. Involvement in sports provides opportunities to challenge themselves and each other both physically and mentally, and builds healthy relationships. Clubs and special interest groups help students bind with like-minded teens and grow cognitively and socially.

However, good education needs financial support, and American schools are increasingly underfunded. As the economy has become more fragile, collection of taxes to support public schools has become more problematic, private schools attract fewer students, and most schools are forced to do more with less. In many districts, something has to give and programs get cut, including sports and most other extracurricular activities. So, the opportunities for the positive influences parents hope schools will exert on their children are becoming more limited. Thus, parents are becoming frustrated.

The nature of education has also changed in many ways. American students are now tested more frequently and more comprehensively than ever before. While the merits and problems of this approach have supporters and critics on both sides, most agree that this increases pressure on students to perform well on these tests, in part because administrative decisions may be based, at least to some degree, on the test results. Students feel the pressure, and they bring it home. Parents then feel the pressure, and it becomes a factor in a complex mix of parents' perception of schools, teachers, and the value of the education their children are receiving.

Parents are also dealing with other influences that increase stress in their lives. As the economy has become more unstable, supporting the family has got more difficult, and more families now must earn more than one income in order to make ends meet. Job security, retirement savings, and leisure time are scarcer. As parents get more hurried, spending time with their kids turns into a challenge, and the distance between parents and their kids grows wider.

Kids also are busier than ever before. Sports and social lives take up much of the awake time of teenagers. Homework increasingly becomes an added pressure. On average, high school students in the United States get assigned 17.5 hours of homework per week, a rate that is higher than many other developed countries. But, this extra work is not translating to more academic success—quite the opposite; the United States continues to fall far below other countries in the percentage of its population graduating from high school. These are widely known facts that further drive the frustration many parents feel toward American schools.

There are also personal factors that must be considered. Parents deal with life stressors and bad relationships. The divorce rate hovers around 50%, as it has now remained for decades. Second marriages are not necessarily better, as divorce rates do not decline with subsequent marriages. Even those parents who stay together frequently experience relationship distress—it's accurately been said that even a good marriage is hard work, and is often filled with day-to-day conflicts. Aging grandparents get sick and need care. Insurance coverage is much more expensive than ever and health care requires much higher out-of-pocket costs that Americans have experienced in the past. Drug prices keep going up, as are our waistlines (in part, because we tend to medicate our stressful lives with high-calorie foods). Life is hard, and parents feel the effects of these pressures.

In this context, we now must ask ourselves: who is a "challenging parent"? This question has many answers, but some of the most common factors have already been mentioned. Challenging parents may be those who deal with many personal stressors, financial pressures, and ailing grandparents. Challenging parents may be those who see their kids losing their innocence because of negative influences all around them, which they, the parents, are desperately trying to outweigh.

Challenging parents may be those who look toward their children's future and realize that maximizing benefits from education, and exposure to many educational opportunities, will improve their children's chances of success, and so they expect (sometimes unreasonably) the schools to do the most they can to help every child (especially theirs). Challenging parents may be those who recognize that their children have special needs, and want schools to attend to those needs to their maximal ability.

Challenging parents may be those who, in their own childhood or adolescence, had a bad experience in school, and therefore do not expect that school will do the most to help their children. And, we must admit, challenging parents may be those who are too busy with their own lives to take much responsibility for their children's education and expect the school to teach their children with little support from home. Thus, the exact mix of factors behind parents' "challenging" attitudes may vary widely.

Still, in the end, most parents and educational professionals strive for the same goal—to help each student grow and learn as much as possible. Thus, although the reasons parents may be "challenging" are so varied, most parents deep down inside really do want to work *with* the school's professionals. This is where the value of this volume becomes so crucial. Understanding the nature of the parents' concerns, their fears and frustrations, as well as their expectations, helps educators learn the context in which the parents' approach toward the school and their children's education is embedded.

A guide such as this helps school professionals understand the nature of the challenge, and, with this understanding, select an approach that connects with the parents' hope for their children while still maintaining the practical (and legal) limits of what interventions and accommodations are available and appropriate. We all want the same goal—for our students and children to succeed. This book helps educators and parents find a way to communicate and work jointly to make that happen.

George M. Kapalka, PhD, MS, ABPP
Board Certified in Clinical Psychology & Psychopharmacology
Certified School Psychologist
Author of:
8 Steps to Classroom Success: A Guide for
Teachers of Challenging Behaviors
Parenting Your Out-of-Control Child
Counseling Boys and Men with ADHD
Nutritional and Herbal Therapies for Children and Adolescents

REFERENCES

* More Sayings by John Sculley View More Sayings and Quotes about Family Sayings. "We Expect Teachers to Handle Teenage Pregnancy, Substance Abuse, and the Failings of the Family. Then We Expect Them to Educate Our Children." Smart Sayings. N.p., 2016. Web. 16 January 2016.

Center for Disease Control and Prevention (2013). *Sexual Risk Behaviors: HIV, STD & Teen Pregnancy Prevention.* Retrieved June 5, 2016 from www.cdc.gov/healthyyouth/sexualbehaviors/

Center for Disease Control and Prevention (2014). *National Survey on Drug Use and Health.* Retrieved June 5, 2016 from http://www.samhsa.gov/data/sites/default/files/NSDUH-FRR1-2014/NSDUH-FRR1-2014.pdf

National Center on Addiction and Substance Abuse (2012). *National Survey on American Attitudes on Substance Abuse XVII: Teens.* Retrieved June 5, 2016 from www.centeronaddiction.org/addiction-research/reports/national-survey-american-attitudes-substance-abuse-teens-2012

National Institute on Drug Abuse (2014). *Drug Facts: High School and Youth Trends.* Retrieved June 5, 2016 from www.drugabuse.gov/publications/drugfacts/high-school-youth-trends

Trust for America's Health (2015). *The Facts Hurt: A State-by-State Injury Prevention Police Report.* Retrieved June 5, 2016 from healthyamericans.org/assets/files/TFAH-2015-InjuryRpt-FINAL.pdf

United States Department of Health and Human Services (2016). *Trends in Teen Pregnancy and Childbearing.* Retrieved June 5, 2016 from www.hhs.gov/ash/oah/adolescent-health-topics/reproductive-health/teen-pregnancy/trends.html

Preface

"If I only had to work with just the kids that would be great ... it is dealing with the parents that is the hard part." I have heard this statement made by more than one exasperated teacher in faculty rooms, conferences, as well as trainings that I have done in numerous districts. These same issues permeate the offices of administrators as they try to perilously climb a wall of parental resistance, anger, and frustration to communicate concerns of discipline and responsibility that often falls on the deaf ears of resistant parents or families drowning in despair and unable to balance one more task without falling under the surface of anxiety and fear.

Please let me be clear, the vast majority of parents and families we work with are helpful, kind, and supportive. These are the parents who we, as educational professionals, are grateful to for their support as they work alongside us, hand in hand, to teach their children how to be the next generation of educated, well-rounded citizens.

This book, however, is not about these parents. This book is about the others. In a 2012 joint survey between the National Education Association and *Parenting* magazine, "68% of teachers reported difficulty dealing with parents."[1] Likewise, in a 2012 MetLife Survey, entitled The MetLife Survey of the American Teacher: Challenges for School Leadership, it was found that more than 7 in 10 educators identify "engaging parents and the community in improving education for students (72% of principals; 73% of teachers) as challenging or very challenging for school leaders."[2]

Parents, especially the difficult ones, are often the greatest advocates for their children and that is a key thread that should be noted and respected throughout this book. Challenging parents may come from challenging situations in their own right. They may have had their own negative educational experiences, or feel that they must resort to aggressive strategies to fight for their children due to what they perceive as a stone wall of an educational system that is troublesome to navigate.

This being said, some parents don't seem to participate at all in the vital work of education for their child. We attempt to entice, beg, and plead with them to be a partner in their child's learning and yet they still maintain a distance by refusing to communicate with the school. What we might not see, however, is a struggle to put food on the table, heat in the home, and lights over their heads. Education is simply not on a radar screen in which you are looking for your next meal or a way to overcome the seemingly unending miles of debt and despondency.

Hopefully, along the journey of this book I will provide you with several tools to add to your tool belt, a chuckle or two, and (most importantly) some better ways to relate with some of the more challenging situations that you encounter with parents, families, and even faculty members in various positions in your school. Most of all, I hope that you find this book to be helpful in the important and vital work that you do in educating our next generation and the many subsequent generations that come through the doors of your school each year. The school is the one and only setting in which the entirety of a generation grows together as a captured audience for educators to make an appreciable difference.

Please accept my heartfelt thanks for allowing me to be a part of your educator family and for spending some time with me in reading this book.

NOTES

1. "Survey Finds Parent-teacher Relationships Strong—Teachers given Grade of." Rss. Accessed April 08, 2016. http://www.nea.org/home/51796.htm.

2. "Work to Implement the CCSS. The MetLife Survey of the ..." Accessed April 8, 2016. http://www.achieve.org/files/March2012Perspective.pdf.

Chapter 1

Introduction

The Climate Change of the School Environment and the Vital Nature of Conflict Resolution Skills for Educators

> The real role of leadership is climate control, creating a climate of possibility.

> —Sir Ken Robinson*

Go into any faculty room of any school, in any district, in any state, and you will hear that educators feel that their very career is under attack. Curriculum standards are changing, expectations are increasing, support is weaning, and the political environment toward the teaching profession is, at times, wavering.

The reason that this is even a chapter in this book is because you must understand the "backstory" that creates a discord among teachers, administrators, and parents that can fuel a proverbial fire, which taints the relational dialogue between parent and educator. Some educators may not hear the tactile myths that swirl around the proverbial "elephant in the room" of what some parents believe. Nevertheless, they are still relevant in understanding and empathizing what is going on when we are sometimes blindsided by parental hostility. These issues are the background music that plays subtly in many interactions within an educational organization.

CLIMATE ISSUE #1: SCHOOL IS WHAT IT WAS WHEN I WAS A STUDENT

Think way back to your kindergarten and primary school years. What you may remember is a muddle of sleep, snack, and recess sprinkled in with some academics for good measure. Flash forward now to the twenty-first century. With increasing emphasis on academics, curriculum, as well as to keep up in the global marketplace, recess and other activities that are of a "nonessential" value are pushed out the door.

Academics now seem to be on hyper drive; what you learned in second grade is likely a similar curriculum to what children learn now in kindergarten. So, what does this have to do with dealing with difficult interactions? If you were not in the educational field you will likely apply your previous knowledge to what your child is learning today.

Statements such as "it is only kindergarten" or "the elementary grades are not important" may pervade a parent's paradigm of the early years of education. This can foster a misunderstanding of "why is the teacher/administrator being so hard on my child" or "why is it necessary to get involved?" To address these issues we must communicate to parents the new world of education that takes place at a frenetic speed. This involves communication, especially with "at risk" parents, about the new world order of public education (more on this later).

CLIMATE ISSUE #2: "I REMEMBER SPECIAL EDUCATION ... I DON'T WANT MY CHILD TO BE IN SPECIAL EDUCATION"

Again, remember that a parent's own history in public education will play an important role in his or her view of their own child's schooling.

If you have a parent who was formerly classified in a special education program only a decade or two ago, he or she is not likely to have a positive viewpoint on the experience of special education for his or her own child. Taking a "small bus" to school; being segregated from his or her peers in a separate classroom; and of some peers snickering, bullying, or pointing him or her out as different are likely to be harsh images emblazed into the parent's memory.

Parents who have had this experience (or those who remember peers that were in this situation) are likely to be very reluctant to discuss the classification of their child or even discuss special education topics with school personnel. They may seem resistant, reluctant, or even hostile, but if we explore their history these memories will rise to the surface.

Use of terms like "least restrictive environment," "classification," and "special transportation" may seem relatively benign. However, to some parents, the mere mention of these words may create fear and anger that close off any further conversation. Such parents must be shown these relatively new special education terms in practice, that is, you must show them what these terms mean visually (rather than merely through words and phrases). To simply discuss these programs is to renew dormant fears of their child being ostracized and to bring up the strong emotional need for them to protect their child from being labeled as "different."

CLIMATE ISSUE #3: "THE SCHOOL SYSTEM DOES NOT LISTEN TO ME AND MY KID'S NEEDS"

As a lifeguard, the first thing they teach you in making a rescue is to be careful when you swim out to people who are drowning; they will try to grab you and pull you under. It is not that the victims intend on hurting you; logic would tell them to relax and let this person bring them to land safely. Emotions, however, tell them this is the only and last desperate hope of their getting in a few additional frantic breaths as their despair and fear of the sea trumps rationality. Or put another way, emotionality and rationality are like mixing oil and water.

Remember, rational and emotional are two very separate things. If you want to speak to a parent rationally listen to him or her emotionally first. As an educator you may think, "Well how do I fix it if I am not offering rational responses to interventions?" Sometimes, just listening and understanding is all the fix the parent may need (more on this later).

CLIMATE ISSUE #4: "I HAVE NOT YET MOURNED MY CHILD'S TRUE ABILITIES"

When you have an oppositional parent/family and they absolutely refuse to accept what you are telling them about their child's abilities (especially in the early primary and elementary grade levels), they may not be ready to hear what you are telling them.

Imagine you are a parent who just had a baby. It is your pride and joy; you have dreams and aspirations of this infant growing up to go to an Ivy League School, becoming a doctor or lawyer, and flourishing in the world around you. Now you tell the parent their child may have some learning or physical disability; it is like hitting an emotional brick wall.

The Kubler-Ross Stages of Grief[1]—denial, anger, bargaining, depression, and acceptance—may need to be waded through. Where and how fast someone goes through them (and in what order) may well determine how well and willing they are to accept your analysis and opinions of what may be needed for their child educationally.

CLIMATE ISSUES #5: "THESE TEACHERS AND ADMINISTRATORS THINK THEY KNOW MY KID ... THE FACT IS, THEY DON'T KNOW HIM/HER AT ALL"

While it is true that we are experienced educational professionals and have spent many years in college, this is not generally important to a parent. As a case in point, how often have you been asked, "Where did you go to school? What is your training? What are the educational theories that you use?"

The fact is parents don't generally ask these questions. Parents assume that you are well educated and trained to teach their child in an appropriate fashion. What they want you to understand is that although you understand children and the education of children, they know their child (at the most visceral level) better than anyone. They want you to know they are the professionals when it comes to their kid. They want you to know they are the ones who raised this special and amazing child. They know their child's habits and idiosyncrasies. They have loved their child and helped him or her grow to where he or she is now. To you their child is a student; to them he or she is their world.

We know this intrinsically. We know how important the bond is between children and parents. The difficulty is that when you speak in terms of abbreviations and educational lingo, parents feel that you are lumping their child with other students. They want their child to be understood as an individual.

This is not to say that we as educators don't comprehend their child as an individual with differentiated learning and instruction. Of course we do. This, however, is not what parents are asking. What they want to know is that you understand the whole picture of their child and what makes them special before (in their frame of mind) you criticize the traits of their son or daughter. Put another way, simply separating the behavior from the child is overly simplistic. Parents want you to know and separate what makes their child special from the behaviors as well and celebrate this before you state anything negative.

CLIMATE ISSUE #6: "BUT MY KID NEEDS ME ... AND I NEED TO BE NEEDED"

Perhaps one of the greatest disservices to our children is that they are being handicapped by a world that tries to coddle them and prevent them from fully outstretching their wings. You see this in parents of children who are chronically absent from school. The first question you ask is, "Is someone home when the child is at school?"

If this is the case, you have an understanding into a potential parental dynamic. If a parent is home, he or she wants the child to keep him or her company. Also, conversely, if the parent is home the child feels that the parent is doing something exciting or picks up the subtle cues that imply "I want you home with me." These mothers and fathers see school as a scary place and want to smother their children in a security blanket of their well-meaning caution.

CLIMATE ISSUE #7: "TEACHERS ARE OVERPAID AND UNDERWORKED"

If you look at the current political environment, it is not very conducive to positive stories about public education. Politicians are trying to navigate the face of public education for political traction while simultaneously throwing under the school bus teachers and the profession of education itself. The salary of educators is stated as greatly inflated to support the fact that they are earning more than their share of the taxpayer dime. This is compounded with the belief that all educators (teachers and administrators are frequently lumped together) have the "cushy jobs" complete with summers off.

At present, union busting (particularly in the teaching industry) is at an all-time high. Teachers unions, pensions, and taxes are all topics of political fodder that leave a negative taste in some parents' mouths and affect educational relationships in a tacit way.

Despite all of this, there is a great silver lining in the clouds. A recent Gallup poll finds the job of educators to be among the top five jobs most respected for their honesty and ethics[2] with only those in medical professions appearing above educators. Still, we must be ever vigilant that conflicted parents will be skeptical so we need to earn their hard-earned trust over what they have heard on the web or local news. It can be, for some parents, an ever-present uphill battle.

CLIMATE ISSUE #8: THE PHYSICAL ENVIRONMENT IS THE FIRST THING PARENTS SEE

The first thing that parents see is the physical environment of the school itself. Parents only get a snapshot glimpse of the whole school building and apply it to their opinion of the school as a whole. They are doing a visual scan and asking: Is this school welcoming? Is the school safe? Does it monitor who comes in and out? Is the front-office staff warm and inviting? Is the building clean or in disrepair?

These questions are answered almost immediately when parents come into the school. They begin to paint a picture of the administrator and educational faculty even before they meet with you. It is their thermometer for school climate so you must try to ensure their quick analysis is a positive one.

Another aspect they consider is your website, the front door of your school on the Internet. When they come to that proverbial front door, they will be looking to see if the information is up to date. If they see holiday decorations and it is spring, it is akin to having holiday decorations up in your hallway in April. Before they have even entered the doors of your school, technology-savvy parents have formed their impression of your school's physical environment based on their vision of your school's virtual environment.

CLIMATE #9: AND SPEAKING OF TECHNOLOGY

Technology is the language of the current and future generations. Computers, smartphones, and the Internet grow at such a frenetic pace that the computer or smartphone you buy today was out of date yesterday. So if our technology is not current in our school it fosters a climate issue. With strict and shrinking budgets there may not be a lot you can do about this. However, parents in the technology field are far less likely to care about a budget crunch and far more likely to blame you for their child not being instilled with the latest and greatest computer skills.[3]

Oftentimes, the technology is only one piece of the puzzle. Some veteran teachers (or even novice teachers) are not as fully versed on the use of technology. Afraid that others have far surpassed them in their aptitude, they simply don't use technology, or they limit its usage. The point is, you can only teach what you know, and if what you know is limited, your ability to teach that subject is limited to the same degree.

Professional development in technology is not likely to net these teachers; it is analogous to taking an advanced course of Japanese when you have only a very rudimentary understanding in the beginner's course. Rather, a one-on-one lesson or a professional development session that offers to help with very basic questions student were afraid to ask will get these teachers involved.

So, getting back to the parent, if the teacher can speak the basics of technology, the parent will be far more confident than a teacher who admits "I am not really into technology." When asked about the types of computer-based programs used in their rooms, such teachers will then feign only a superficial knowledge. Our students as well as our brains are changing. Here's an example to support this fact: ten years ago you would be able to tell me the phone numbers of your family and friends, you would be able to give me directions or read a map. Today, smartphones have replaced the need for these past skill sets. Ignorance of technology will no longer be tolerated by challenging parents, nor should it.

CLIMATE #10: AN UNINFORMED PARENT IS NOT YOUR BEST CUSTOMER

Parents who do not recognize policies, procedures, or curriculum in your school are more apt to be challenging parents, as they are surprised by information that they either were not aware of or never took the time to look at. Therefore, if you have information you want parents to understand, ensure that it is written or printed on a piece of paper that they will have to sign and return so you have documentation of their reviewing materials.

Keep websites updated with the latest information and encourage your teachers to have regular contact with parents. Advise them to make an especially concerted effort for challenging parents who are likely to grow frustrated and come into your office in a huff after they simmer and become irritated. Start off with a call for a positive reason.

CLIMATE ISSUE #11: WHAT IS YOUR FAULT ... IS YOUR FAULT WHAT IS NOT YOUR FAULT ... IS YOUR FAULT

This is an unfortunate by-product of being an educator. As an educational leader no matter what happens in the school, the larger politics of the educational system, or any other item, ultimately becomes your issue and, in turn, according to the parent's perspective "your fault." There is no sense in disagreeing with this or playing the role of the martyr; this is just a natural by-product of being a leader (or an educator for that matter). A greater number of social roles are being heaped on to the already overflowing plates of public education.

CLIMATE ISSUE #12: STUDENT AND FAMILY POVERTY ISSUES

With students, we discuss the concept of fair not being equal, but everyone getting what they need—not necessarily what they want. Although this is an admirable adage, it is not true in the world for many of our students and their families. In many cases, impoverished families cannot make education a priority simply because other basic items for survival are far more necessary such as food, water, clothing, and shelter. True, some parents have issues that they bring upon themselves by way of alcohol or drugs; however, in the end, what matters is what we do to ultimately help the child.

Later in this book we will discuss how to involve "at risk" parents. These are the parents we are primarily talking about. Those that do not attend parent-teacher association (PTA) meetings, whose phone numbers change so often we cannot keep one that is current in our records, and who (when you do find the correct number) don't call back.

Still, it is important to recognize this as a school climate issue. If you work in an affluent district don't think that you are spared. Sometimes parents are only a paycheck away from losing a home or in low-income areas of your town. Parents routinely struggle to balance losing heat, electricity, and water utility services.

Here are some thoughts on dealing with the climate issue of poverty within your school environment:

- *Work as a partner with local social services, community, and civic organizations:* Having a good working relationship with these groups and people can become enormously helpful in supporting families in need.
- *Don't expect a thank you:* Sometimes, we expect parents to give us a degree of gratitude for what we do to support a family. We think "Well, if they aren't thanking us why should we bother to continue to help?" Unfortunately, when a family has the weight of the world on their shoulders, sometimes the thought of expressing gratitude, in the haste of an urgent situation, evaporates in the specter of the next crisis.
- *Bring the school to them:* If you have a social worker or counselor in your school, consider having them go to the family. Of course, this should be done with caution and faculty should always go partnered with someone else. However, if you want to meet parents, sometimes you must simply meet them where they are, even if it is not within the realm of your school.
- *Don't judge:* Oftentimes, you will hear skeptical faculty or other parents saying, "Well, if they are so poor why does she get her nails done? Why do they have cable TV? Why do they have that car?" The bottom line is we do not know a family's true financial situation, and we are only there to assist the student to learn. Any obstacles we remove will, hopefully, filter down to the student, who we know has absolutely no control over the situation at hand.

CLIMATE ISSUE #13: STANDARDIZED TESTING, CORE CURRICULUM STANDARDS, AND ALL THAT

Parents have a great deal of misconceptions about standardized testing and Common Core curriculum standards. Their opinions range from "they are not important" to "they will determine a child's very future livelihood and career." Again, this is a case in which having a little information can prove to be a dangerous thing.

It is critical, therefore, to provide accurate information in a user-friendly format to parents regarding core curriculum, standardized testing, and the like, to avoid misconceptions spinning out of control to mammoth proportions. Usually, searching the web for frequently asked questions or developing a list of questions that are asked to you and your peers will nip in the bud any fearful rumors or gossip and quell others that are not addressed outright.

CLIMATE #14: WHAT IS GOING OUT REPRESENTS WHAT IS COMING IN TO THE CLIMATE OF YOUR SCHOOL AND CAN'T BE TAKEN BACK

In a related event, the *New York Daily News* on February 19, 2016, reported that a public school in Delaware was given a black eye because they had unintentionally sent out a "Hurt Feelings Report" in which it sarcastically satires that the purpose of the document is to "assist whiners in documenting hurt feelings." It went on to say "Whiners should use this form to seek sympathy from someone who cares."[4]

The school district quickly replied, "This was an embarrassing mistake, but it was just that—a mistake." This mistake, however, is an important lesson that we can all learn. It is too easy to hit send on an e-mail and let it go. You are also at the discretion of the faculty who are exponentially sending e-mails back and forth from parents, engaging in social media, etc. It is worth having a meeting to address appropriate e-mails, restrictions to social media, and when to use e-mail dialogue with faculty. Sometimes, common sense is not so common when it comes to the line being blurred in terms of humor and digital communications.

CLIMATE #15: "THIS SCHOOL IS FULL OF BULLIES AND MY CHILD IS BEING BULLIED"

Bullying has always seemed a rite of passage; if you have watched movies and television programs over the years, many of them allude to bullying. They take a lighthearted look at bullying and are the source of many laughs on both the big and small screen alike.

Flash forward to the Internet age; now we have bullying taking on a life of its own as cyberbullying enables a small seed of bullying to "go viral" and spread like wildfire over the Internet through messaging, or the plethora of other Internet means. With extensive media coverage, bullying has now gone from a rite of passage, to a school disciplinary issue, to a series of serious laws that districts must follow nationwide.

This being said, parents are extra vigilant for any behavior in the school environment that even smacks of traces of bullying. With this newfound sensitivity to the prospective long- and short-term harm that can be caused to a child's fragile psyche, parents come into school ready to defend their child, tooth and nail, from a school climate that is harsh and prospectively harmful to him or her.

As you well know, the long-term and lasting effects of bullying are harmful without any doubt. It only takes thinking back to your middle school days and you can remember the names and faces of those that bullied you and made your existence in school a miserable one. Now, imagine the frustration if you storm into your child's school as a parent only to be told that what is going on for your child, though traumatic, is not classified as a bullying incident?

The anger and blood-boiling is palpable as you think the school does not take the advocacy of your child seriously. Unfortunately, however, what many parents see as bullying cannot be classified, in the legal sense and definition, as harassment, intimidation, or bullying. Rather, they are disciplinary issues that may be handled in much the same way without the label being applied to the dubious behavior(s).

To avoid this confusion, it is important that a definition based on your state's interpretation of bullying be made clear to each parent that is within your school. To further assist in this climate issue, consider the following:

- *Have students and parents sign an antibullying clause/pledge:* This pledge defines what bullying is, and is not, as well as the clearly spelled out consequences for an infraction.
- *Focus on targets as well as the aggressor:* Many antibullying programs are heavily focused on the aggressor and have little or no emphasis on the victim. In such cases, the target is often victimized again and again each year by a different bully for the same behaviors. Assertiveness is the key to teaching both aggressive and passive students to reach a middle ground.
- *Parenting programs that focus on bullying are important because bullying can start in the home:* If I have older siblings who pick on me and I am powerless to fight back, I am likely to bring that frustration and anger to a place where I can find someone who is equally powerless to my situation—namely the school setting. Also, many of the harassment, intimidation, and bullying situations that occur now begin outside of school via the Internet or through texting, and then spill over into school making it a school issue as well. Therefore, equipping parents is a good fail-safe for beginning to address a problem before it boils out of control and into the academic environment.
- *Believe the students:* As you already know, children are smart and can be devious; bullying does not occur in front of the eyes of the teacher. It occurs in the dark corners of recess, lunch, the locker room, or even the bathrooms. Therefore, the teachers and administration are often the last to know. This is especially true with girls who are experts at isolating a weaker girl and proverbially freezing her out of any relationship. This means we have to put an ear to these environments especially. It means listening to students when they are talking (or not talking) and having your counselor do informal groups like a "lunch bunch" in which students feel comfortable enough to discuss the true school climate versus what they think educators want to hear the school is like.

CLIMATE #16: THE BOTTOM LINE ...
FACE IT, MAYBE IT IS YOU

Each day the role of an educator or administrator is chock-full of responsibilities. Between curriculum, parenting, faculty, and, not to mention, personal issues, we have very little time to self-reflect.

Sometimes, the hardest thing to do is to simply accept responsibility. When our ego gets in the way of our learning how to improve, we stall. The world is chock full of political, administrative, managerial, and a host of other jobs in which responsibility is sloughed off to another person or circumstance. In so doing, opportunities to learn and improve go out the proverbial windows of the many corner offices that were earned by hard and tireless work.

Are the personality habits that we engage in each day indicative of an educational leader or are they a direct obstacle to what can make us an effective educator and, in turn, the best suited at handling conflictual issues accordingly?

Here is the top ten list of situations that could impair or enhance your ability to handle tough discussions or issues in an appropriate fashion:

1. *Resistance to change:* If you do not accept that your faculty and the dynamics from a number of factors are going to change, you will tend to always be irritated and frustrated. The one thing we can always expect is change: either accept it and its flow or run upstream and exhaust yourself. You cannot be at your best for parents or faculty in a perpetually exhausted state.

2. *Making your decision with your heart as opposed to your head:* It is important to be caring and emotional toward your job. However, when you use your heart over your head with everything, you become inconsistent and the faculty, as well as all those that you interact with, learn that your decisions will be based on how you feel for the day. Reactions then are at a knee jerk–based emotional or energy-dependent level.

   As an example, when you get on an airplane you hear the calm and unemotional voice of the pilot. His monotone and unchanging voice is soothing and you slump into your seat relaxed that the flight will be safe and uneventful. Now, imagine he gets on the airplane intercom and you sense tense emotion in his voice. No matter what he says you will be distrustful and worried about your safety. His voice and emotion determines your sense of his control of the situation. Likewise, if you are using your head versus your heart your faculty, parents, as well as students will feel safe and they will have a good degree of predictability in their relationship to you.

3. *Control monger:* If you feel you must have control over everything you will find that you will have control over nothing. Decide what you should

have control over and let the other parts go. How does this effect parent relationships?

Here are the things *you cannot* control:

- What a parent does at home.
- What a parent and family does not have at home.
- What a parent or student thinks of you (to a varying degree).
- Homework, tutoring.
- New curriculum, technology, (or lack thereof) and changes implemented at the local, state, or federal level.
- A host of many other things that would fill a book in itself.

4. *Inability or unwillingness to make decisions:* If you are the kind of person who constantly waits or has difficulty making decisions, parents will become frustrated and certain types of parents will attempt to push you into making a snap decision. Eventually, you are forced to make a decision when the fire is out of control. It is better to put out the small brush fire than the raging inferno of a wildfire.

5. *Not having notable visions or values:* Should you be someone who is trying to struggle day to day in your position, you will be unable to "see the forest for the trees" or to develop a short-term or long-term vision for your school and your relationships with the stakeholders. It is like trying to think about how you can better mediate when you are trying to focus on getting your next gasp of air while drowning.

   The problem when you don't have vision is that you cannot have a discussion with parents and know what the constraints or boundaries are that you have and won't negotiate on.

6. *Admission of mistakes:* In a leadership role you will make plenty of mistakes. Unfortunately, the mistakes will affect students, parents, and faculty in many cases. If you are someone that holds stubbornly onto your decisions even if they are wrong and then become angered when they are pointed out, this will melt away your credibility with all parties that come into interaction with you. Admit mistakes quickly, repair what you can, and move on without beating yourself up.

7. *Anger, the worst emotion of all:* Anger has its place in leadership; it can get your point across clearly when you need to. This being noted, however, if you use anger too often people stop listening. They hear you but they stop listening as they realize you are nothing but a blowhard who spouts every hour like the geyser Ole Faithful.

   The other, and larger, concern is that if you are directed by extreme anger you get a tunnel vision–type response to things. If you think about the last time you were cut off on the highway when you may have cursed out that "crazy driver," you would also realize that, in your lack of vision, you did not know who else was in the car who may have heard your expletive-flavored rant. Why is this? This is because when you have been in the midst of that haze of rage you have forgotten the effect it has on those around you—including the extremely impressionable five-year-old in the backseat. What would happen if you apply this dangerous precedent to how you handle school situations?

8. *I am better than them:* This is an easy one. You are the leader but you are no better or worse than anyone in the school or any of the clients of the school. If you think you are or judge others because of the situation they are in, you cannot simultaneously empathize and help those that need you in a capable fashion.

9. *Playing favorites and the "us versus them" attitude:* We all have favorites; favorite students, faculty members, and parents. If you acknowledge that we all have this bias, it will go a long way toward your trying your best to stay clear of it (or making it blatantly obvious).

10. *Pointing fingers at others:* As the saying goes, if you point a finger at someone else there are four more fingers pointing directly back at you. The bottom line is, you are the leader and the buck stops with you. So, if you blame someone else, not only are you not solving the problem, but you also are losing a modicum of respect among those that you are leading each time you do so.

CLIMATE #17: BELIEF OF THE FALLACY OF PUBLIC EDUCATION BEING "FAIR"

Often parents expect "fair" in schools to mean "equal." They believe that their child should be treated the exact same way as their neighbor's child. However, this is usually a double-edged sword; parents want their child to be treated the same when it is something that they feel they are entitled to and different if it is something that is negative or punitive in nature.

The truth is, there is no way that a school system can do things equally. Meaning, they cannot treat all students exactly the same. Different schools have varying budgets and in the very classes of those schools we have differentiated instruction providing more services for special education students than traditional students, on the same taxpayer dime.

Now, parents may point out that "it is unfair" that one student gets a certain intervention, service, disciplinary consequence, etc., while the other does not. We must let them know of a more reasonable and logical means of applying equitable education to a diverse group of students.

When explaining education, it is necessary first for them to understand that due to privacy concerns we do not discuss individual students. Further, in education, we give a child what he or she needs and not what is wanted. In explaining this to a parent, We tailor a child's education (in our school) to what a child needs and each of our children have different and diverse needs.

CLIMATE #18: THE MYTH OF NONJUDGMENT

As educators we must face a fact that we are all judgmental. Often, we try to pretend that we do not have favorite students, parents, or faculty. Or, that students and parents do not have a negative (or positive) history that is almost solely based on the judgment of past educators when they come into the doors of our school. We try to encourage parents (and ourselves) that students (and parents) arrive at school with "a clean slate" and that we will form our own judgments. This is often well-intentioned but not always realistic.

It may not be fair, or right, or what we think is our best professional or personal self. Honesty, however, goes a long way in making appreciable change than not acknowledging this sad fact. It allows us to put the issue on the table, and say we must temper our opinion with that of what we were told.

NOTES

* "12 Profound Quotes by Sir Ken Robinson on Creativity." Best Masters in Education. Accessed February 16, 2016. http://www.bestmastersineducation. com/12-quotes-by-sir-ken-robinson-on-creativity/.

1. "Family Grief." *Counselling for Grief and Bereavement Counselling for Grief and Bereavement.* 55–79. doi:10.4135/9781446214800.n4.

2. Carr, Jelleff C. "Gallup Poll Rates Honesty and Ethical Standards." *Regulatory Toxicology and Pharmacology* 29, no. 1 (1999): 96. doi:10.1006/rtph.1998.1284.

3. "How Blaming Teachers Shortchanges Students - NEA Today." NEA Today. 2012. Accessed February, 2016. http://neatoday.org/2012/11/26/how-blaming-teachers-shortchanges-students-2/.

4. Hanna, Laurie. "Delaware Parents Angry after School Accidentally Sends out 'Hurt Feelings Report' They Say Mocks Bullying." *New York Daily News* 19 Feb. 2016. Web.

Chapter 2

Know Thyself

The Importance of Knowing Your Own Conflict Management Style and That of Others

Know Thyself.

—Socrates*

As Publilius Syrus once said, "Anyone can hold the helm when the sea is calm." Being captain of a school can be easy if the seas are tranquil and you keep the steering wheel straight. It is when the waters start churning, the storm clouds seem foreboding, and the lightning is the only thing to light your way that times get difficult. Needless, to say these are also the times that are most trying in your interactions when the waters get choppy in a situation with a challenging parent or family.

KNOW YOURSELF

Be honest with yourself. Know who you are, your personality, as well as your potential strengths and weaknesses. The fact is you may be better at handling certain types of conflicts, personalities, and situations than others. All of us come with a unique set of abilities and weaknesses. If you are aware of both, you can prepare for what may be your Achilles' heel; those kinks in your armor that you are not as prepared for or that catch you off guard.

This starts with an understanding of your conflict resolution style. We all have one that is our dominant strategy we tend to cling to. It is likely to have served us and our personality type well; however, we are also likely to recognize that it does not always match the diverse set of issues, personalities, and problems that are laid before us as educational leaders.

15

CONFLICT AVOIDER STYLE

Most of us do not like conflict. At the first sign of argument, conflict avoiders tend to become visibly uncomfortable and do anything they can to set the situation right so as to avoid any discord. This can mean agreeing to things they do not agree on in principle. Other tactics that parallel this include simply walking away, avoiding the topic, using lighthearted humor to take the sting out of the issue, or even not seeing the proverbial elephant in the room. The theory is, "If I don't address the issue, the problem will hopefully burn itself out" like a campfire that runs out of wood to fuel itself.

Sometimes this can be acceptable and even a good strategy. Not everything needs to be a fight or an argument, and if everything did end in this manner, we would quickly burn out and our schools would stall and fail. However, when it comes to certain matters, your lack of action can lead to more serious and dire consequences, now or in the future.

If you are a conflict avoider, you must ask yourself:

- *Is this a problem worth fighting for?* If it is, you cannot avoid it.
- *Is this an issue that will cause a safety concern now or later?* If so, it must be handled now.
- *Does this predicament directly conflict against my values as an educator and my vision?* If it does, you must confront it sooner rather than later.
- *What will the result of my backing off of this problem create?* If you back off of a conflict you may safely expect that the parent/family is going to view this as an invite to take a step forward. This means that setting up a boundary later may be more difficult in a secondary, more serious, dispute, should one arise.

"I WANT TO BE FRIENDS WITH EVERYONE" STYLE

Nobody likes to be on the side of the stick in which they have the reputation of being a "jerk," "bastard," or "bitch" (excuse the language but this is what we are truly being labeled as). We want to be friends with everyone: students, faculty, and parents. However, this becomes an issue when we eventually, at some point, get backed into a wall and suddenly find ourselves between a rock and a hard place and fight or further attack are the only two options.

It is noble to want to not rock the boat of the community that is your school; however, again you must ask yourself the following:

- *Am I becoming a martyr?* If you try to be friends with everyone, then certain people will start to take advantage. They will realize not how far they can push you, but rather, that you are a "pushover." When they do so, you will begin to feel victimized by the very people you are trying to help.

- *Is my role being questioned?* When you are friends with everyone it blurs the lines of your role. Parents begin to feel too comfortable and begin to take steps that they assume would be okay because you are friendly. In your conflict style, a distinction must be made between being "friendly" and being "friends."
- *Are they a friend or enemy?* If you are trying to be friends and help everyone, there is a very real tendency to begin to classify those parents who do not buy into your friendliness as enemies. In reality, there are very few friends and enemies. Rather, there are shades of gray on a spectrum of acquaintances. It is better to not take anything personally that you deem overly positive or negative among your interactions with parents and their opinions as such.

"YOU'RE GOING TO LISTEN AND FOLLOW WHAT I SAY OR ELSE" STYLE

We all have had bosses like this one—they tell you what you are going to do, should do, and how to do it. There is only one way to do something; their way—that is the right and only way. They divide scenarios into "winning" and "losing" and encourage fighting to be a winner. If you are on their team you must, and will, win, whatever the costs to anyone and everyone.

If your personality style tends to lean toward this direction it is important to consider the following:

- *There is often more than one way to do something*: If you are competitive in nature, you will often tend to think your way is the right way. You will miss the quiet voices in the room that may not be as forceful as you, but that may have good ideas. Hold your idea, your voice, and listen.
- *Harder does not mean better*: Being loud with parents or forceful of your opinion does not necessarily mean they will embrace your ideas more readily than through quiet discussions.
- *There are not always "winners" and "losers"*: If you have offended or shut down a relationship by being too forceful, no one wins. If you are having problems with parents, try to think in terms of "win-win." If they lose, you lose. If you lose, they lose.
- *There is a time for you to use this strategy*: If there is an issue of safety, then your conflict style could be of great use. Therefore, if you see a parental issue in which a child or parent is put at risk due to safety concerns, do not hesitate. This is the time to let your natural conflict resolution strategy

shine. There is no room for gray areas. All involved need to know that with safety there is a very real "win/lose" dynamic.

"LET'S FIGURE THIS ALL OUT TOGETHER" STYLE

If there is a best means of addressing conflict, this is probably it. In this conflict you try to work hand in hand with the parent to find a resolution that is mutually satisfactory. This means that you try to make a compromise that positively affects the student, school, and educators in a collaborative fashion.

Regardless of whether your personality for conflict resolution is to cooperate with others, you must be careful not to "cooperate" certain elements of your disagreement away.

For instance:

- *Do not cooperate your values away*: It is advantageous to cooperate on issues that a student or parent may be having within a school. However, you must have a strong, grounded set of values, visions, and principles so that you know how far you are willing to compromise within your given set of boundaries. In this way, you can cooperate and adjust needs accordingly, but not when they exit out of the bounds of your values.
- *Be certain, cooperate means we work together*: When you are cooperating with parents, be certain they understand that this means they will work together with you. This means action from both educators and parents. This will not generally work among unmotivated or very overwhelmed parents, as it will require an equal (or close to equal) amount of energy on their part. It is likely, although they may not say it, that they just don't have that 50% to give. Therefore, don't expect it, because if you do, you may just lead yourself to disappointment and an ineffective resolution.
- *It does not mean that one side pulls everything to their side and is declared the winner*: It means we equally row the boat together toward the destination. It also means we should never work harder than the other interested party (namely, the parents).

"CAN'T WE JUST FIND A SOLUTION HERE" STYLE?

If you are the kind of person who tries to find a compromise, this is you. If you figure there has got to be a half-way mark that we can reach and be satisfied, then this is your problem solution style. You are someone who believes in "give and take" and characterizes that although life isn't fair, school should be a utopia that is as close to this ideal as possible.

The ultimate goal of this style is to find a solution in which both parties feel they have taken away something positive: a virtual "win-win." It is important to remember that by using this style it does not mean that you give in to your values or reject what is best for the student; it means everyone gets some of what they want. The goal is to make everyone as satisfied as possible.

This often is another good strategy of resolution in your inventory. That being said, as we will discuss below, it is not the best strategy to use with all parents as, just like the others, this conflict resolution style also has its limitations.

COMPROMISING-STYLE-OF-CONFLICTS STYLE

In not looking for a "win-win" solution, you prefer to give some and lose some in this style of conflict resolution. The difficulty with this style is that you are not seeking a winning collaboration for all involved. Rather, you are looking to push and pull what you want and what you are willing to give up to a middle ground that is hopeful for all. The challenge here is a topic in which you cannot meet anywhere near the middle of an issue.

THE CONFLICT RESOLUTION SPECTRUM

We all have tools that we use to get what we want. Look at your children when you go shopping. If they want to get a toy they may scream, throw tantrums, plead, beg, try to suck up to you, or use any of a number of tools from the belt of childhood behaviors to convince you to resolve this conflict so that they can have a toy proudly dangling from their little hands.

They quickly learn, from sifting through these tools, what works and what does not. If sucking up does not work with mom, they quickly transition to begging. If this fails, perhaps asking dad may get them what they want. When all else fails, an all-out tantrum may be the answer. The point is, children quickly assess a situation, adapt, and respond with the correct skill for the right situation.

Likewise, if you are going to handle the myriad of situational conflicts that occur, you must know your preferred conflict management styles and how they fit into the issues you will be addressing.

Our conflict management skills all exist along a continuum between passivity and aggression. Some of us are more passive, which leads us to not address issues with others as readily. We sometimes do not address issues of conflict as quickly as we should for fear of angering the parent, faculty member, or other party. This causes us to turn our anger inward as we kick ourselves for failing to handle the issue or for sidestepping it all together. When anger is turned inward, this could lead to depression.

On the other side is aggression. We have all had very memorable supervisors who used aggression as the means to handle conflict. These were the people whose veins bulged out of their head as they screamed and yelled as a matter of course. In order to get their point across, and to win over an issue, they would yell louder and intimidate their way through winning a conflict.

Then, there is the assertive personality that represents a balance of the two extremes. In an assertiveness style, you do not allow yourself to be a proverbial doormat, but you also do not rise to the level of bullying to get your point across. In this strategy you do not try to avoid the attention of a conflict (as in a passive strategy) nor do you attempt to monopolize all the attention (as in an aggressive paradigm).

AGGRESSIVE STYLE

Belief: "The louder and more forceful you are the more people will listen and respect you."

Result: People either immediately fight back, flee, or do not give you much needed information for fear of a blow up.

Problem with this style: Aggression leads to a lack of respect for boundaries, and you will frequently step over the line in conflicts.

Best time for this conflict style: In an emergency or a clear cut safety issue where roles and boundaries need to firm and implemented.

ASSERTIVE STYLE

Belief: "I am willing to address and compromise on issues with you within reason."

Result: People will begin to recognize that they must respect boundaries, rules and roles; however they will be listened to and respected.

Problem with this style: In cases of emergency you may not have time to negotiate. In minor issues it may just be better to save your conflict resolution skills for bigger issues.

PASSIVE STYLE

Belief: "It is better to be nice...kill them with kindness and avoid conflict at all costs."

Result: People will either not understand where the boundaries and values that they should not cross are or take advantage.

Problem with this style: Conflicts become a never ending series of giving in to others to avoid escalation. In the end, you are left angry at yourself for being walked over and maybe forced to adopt an aggressive stance eventually when your back is against the wall from once you cannot say "yes" any further.

So which one are you? How far do you lean to one side or another in a conflict? You may know your intelligence quotient (IQ) and maybe even your emotional intelligence quotient (EQ) but what of your conflict resolution quotient (CQ)?

Formally, there may not be such a descriptor as a conflict resolution quotient; however, you must have a significant awareness as to what your abilities, strengths, and preferences are for solving problems if you are going to be an effective problem and conflict resolver.

These screenings (see appendices) are just an opportunity for you to get a basic idea of the means you use to resolve conflict. Is one style better than another? Well, it would depend on the issue that you are addressing. It is best, however, to know what you have within your abilities in terms of conflict resolution and to stretch to develop other skills for handling problems outside of your comfort zone. As the old saying goes, "If you only have a hammer then everything looks like a nail."

If you have more tools you will recognize that maybe hammering this particular conversation is not the best way to handle it. Perhaps, developing additional tools and strengths in another area will then allow you to be more effective in dealing with a conflict. The alternative is to continue to use the same tools you have used over and over and get the limited results that you have always got. For all assessments, please refer to the appendices at the end of the book.

NOTE

* By All Means Marry; If You Get a Good Wife, You'll Become Happy; If You Get a Bad One, You'll Become a Philosopher." "Socrates Quotes (Author of Essential Thinkers - Socrates)." Socrates Quotes (Author of Essential Thinkers - Socrates). Accessed February 23, 2016. http://www.goodreads.com/author/quotes/275648. Socrates.

Chapter 3

Maybe It Is YOU!

The Moment You Take Responsibility for Everything in Your Life is the Moment You Can Change Anything in Your Life.

—Hal Elrod*

BOTTOM LINE … FACE IT, MAYBE IT IS YOU

Look in the mirror … you have a difficult job. As you become inundated with responsibilities it is easy to forget an important aspect of success. One must look inward and reflect on what is truly within one's locus of control as well as to what extent one can change them.

Sometimes, the hardest thing to do is to simply accept responsibility. When our ego gets in the way of our learning of how to improve, we stall. The world is chock-full of political, administrative, managerial, and a host of other jobs in which responsibility is sloughed off to another person or circumstance. In so doing, opportunities to learn and improve go out the proverbial windows of the many corner offices that were built by hard and tireless work.

1. *Fear and procrastination and lack of priorities of such:*
   Like the "inability to make decisions" discussed above, when we are afraid, like when we are angry, we delay. We worry and ruminate over small, minor details or issues and fail to react to the larger ones that need to be handled. In short, we become a "pro" at "procrastination."

   When you worry about, "what if (fill in the blank) happens?" the very next question you must ask yourself is what are the chances? You may

be afraid of lightning and yet the chances of being struck are so astro-
nomically low that you probably are better off not daydreaming about it
when you are crossing the road and dealing with the (far greater) risk of
getting hit by a car.

   If you are going to address worry you must deal with it "head on."
Delaying or putting a parent or faculty member off indefinitely only
causes the issue(s) to grow to a point that is as bad, or worse, than you
initially imagined it to be. Dealing head on with issues will allow you to
put your "head on" your pillow at night without issue.

2. *Not listening:* If you are listening to a parent or faculty member
   halfheartedly, then you are not listening. People can inherently tell when
   you are pretending to listen instead of actually making an attempt to
   understand where they are coming from. When you don't listen to others,
   you may find they will force you to listen by their action or inaction. Take
   the time to listen; if you can't, don't simply hear them out.

3. *Not being able to say "no":* Many times we equate the word "no" from
   someone as being rejected or just "being plain mean." Further, as educators, we are hesitant to say "no" to peers, parents, and others for the fear
   of not appearing to be a team player. When you don't say no, you open
   yourself up to halfheartedly saying "yes" to many things you are not able,
   willing, or capable of doing. You will end up resentful of others and, in
   turn, become overwhelmed. We cannot take on other's work if we are not
   at our best to handle our own tasks.

4. *"Feeling bad":* At times we allow guilt to drive a majority of our decisions. How many times do you say, "I feel bad" about the host of issues
   you come in contact with? You must understand that it is important to be
   empathetic and to change what you can; however, when guilt rules your
   decisions it does not allow you to make a balanced judgment. Additionally, negative emotion wears you down like a rock smoothed by a raging
   river. Ultimately, over time, this leads to fatigue and eventual burnout.
   Instead of stating "I feel bad" ask "Can I change this and, if so, how?"
   Should your answer be that you cannot alter or change a situation, recognize this and place your energies elsewhere.

5. *Laugh at yourself:* If you look around in your typical school day you will
   see humor. If you laugh at yourself and don't take everything you do
   seriously it will keep you from "burning out" or being known as taking
   yourself "too seriously."

6. *Asking yourself "what if?"* Asking yourself "what if?" is okay if you
   are seeking to be proactive in making a choice. However, it becomes a
   problem when one endlessly ruminates over the "what ifs" to a point of
   decision paralysis. When asking "what if" questions, you must pair them
   with "what are the chances" of each potential situation occurring. This will

provide an adequate balance and prevent you from falling into a perpetual trap of worry, fear, and procrastination.

7. *Stay away from drama:* We all know fellow faculty (and family) members who stoke the fire of negativity or drama. When we make choices we should stay away from these people as they will make it difficult to make a decision that has an equal amount of emotion as well as logic.

8. *Write it down:* Many times, as we allow emotions to cycle around our brains over and over again, we become overwhelmed. If we look inside our minds, we would find that we are not overthinking. Rather, we are milling the same few thoughts in our heads over and over. Write them down (especially at night if they keep you awake) and try to write down solutions. Concurrently, writing down a list of positives and negatives for each choice has been a true and time-tested method of deciding between two potential convergent tasks.

Whatever decision is made, keep in mind that no decision is set in stone. If you are making a wrong move, try to recognize and change it immediately (versus allowing your pride or stubbornness to continue down the wrong pathway). Monitor and listen to criticism and change your track if what you are hearing is valid. Seek the opinions of peers you trust will provide you with open and honest criticism, not just those who answer "yes" to your questions or statements because that is merely what they think you might want to hear.

NOTE

* By Choosing Your Purpose in Life – a Purpose That Serves the Greater Good – and Devoting the Majority of Your Time, Energy, and Attention Everyday toward Living It, You Discover the Secret to a Life of Fulfillment. "Inspiring Quotes | Successful Habits | Your Morning Routine." HalElrod.com. Accessed March 9, 2016. http://halelrod.com/quotes/.

Chapter 4

Building the Foundation

Making Sure You Are on Firm Footing before You Climb the Mountain of a Challenging Conversation

> Whenever you're in conflict with someone there is one factor that can make the difference between damaging your relationship or deepening it. That factor is attitude.
>
> —William James*

Imagine for a moment that some people come to your home unannounced. They throw open the doors and then begin to mercilessly criticize what you do, how you care for your children, and what your priorities are, while also claiming that you neglect working with your children.

You sit there openmouthed and stunned for a minute and then you start becoming angry. Who are they to judge me and my child? I did not even invite them into my home or my life and now they claim to know more about what is right for me and my child? How dare they!

Now, you may be saying this is not the way that I approach working with the parents or families in my district. I take a positive and collaborative approach and would never think to reach out to a family in this way. Yet, a family's history with school systems goes far beyond their initial interaction with you. It is a long extended and complicated history that may even extend back generations. Therefore, it is important you build a foundation as an educator and advocate for their child as early as possible.

THE WRINKLED HEART THEORY ... WHAT YOU CAN'T TAKE BACK

One of the most effective lessons for students on forgiveness is a simple one; cut two identical hearts out of paper. Now, the students are encouraged after a discussion of the effectiveness of forgiveness and apologies to hurl insults at one of the hapless paper hearts. Simultaneously, they are asked to wrinkle, stomp, and otherwise desecrate the same paper heart.

Next, they are asked to apologize profusely at the inanimate piece of paper, confessing all that they said and trying to provide the sincerest apologies possible. Finally, one of the students is asked to take the wrinkled, ripped heart and make it as "good as new" like the unscathed identical paper heart that was set aside.

Despite their very best efforts of trying to smooth, tape, and otherwise repair the heart, it is never quite the same. And so it is when you say something without thinking to a parent or faculty member. Once it comes out of your mouth, no amount of forgiveness will smooth the wrinkles, creases, and tears you put in the delicate relationships you have with those around you. People have strong memories and tend to remember the negatives much longer and more deeply than the positives.

BUT ... DON'T BE AFRAID OF THE "ELEPHANT IN THE ROOM"

Sometimes we let fear dictate meetings. We know what needs to be said but we are all afraid to say it. Maybe it is because we are afraid of hurting the parent or causing an emotional explosion but we don't say what really needs to be said to move a meeting and situation forward. Whether it is an intervention, a concern, a behavior—whatever it is—we dance around "the elephant," we talk around "the elephant," we hint about "the elephant," but we don't say what needs to be said.

If an issue must be brought up, it must be done directly. This is not to say that there is ever a reason to be hurtful, exploitative, or intentionally confrontational with a parent or family; just that we must not be afraid to broach a topic only because we are fearful and would rather skirt the issue.

This being noted, there are certainly some faculty members who are more tactful and can temper empathy with directness, and these are the ones who should be selected for this job. These faculty members (we all have them on our staff) can approach a topic like skillful surgeons and attack an issue directly while leaving the remainder of the emotional fragility of a family as unscathed as possible.

USING VERBAL JUDO

As a practitioner of the martial art of Judo for many years, this is a technique that has bearing in Far Eastern Culture. In Judo, unlike sports such as wrestling, you are matched up against opponents based on belt and rank rather than size. This can theoretically mean that a skinny 5-foot-8-inch person could be equally matched with an opponent well over 6 feet tall and tipping the scales at 230 pounds.

One might say that this is certainly not an even match, not by a long shot! The power and strength of the larger opponent could overpower the evidently weaker opponent in a second, or so it would seem at least. However, this martial art does not count on brawn or power, but technique.

So how does this relate to conflict skills in the educational arena? Good question. It teaches us that when we go up verbally against a parent, faculty member, or anyone for that matter, it is not about exerting our power and advantage. Rather, it is about using a technique that does not involve showing power or staging a contest to prove who's right and why.

We know that if someone is "right" in a conversation it often simply does not matter. If you "win" a conversation by proving by a preponderance of evidence that the other is abundantly wrong, how much satisfaction will you get and for how long? It will likely be short-lived because although your point may be right in the court of logic, in the realm of the emotional toll you will come up extremely short and develop resentment from the other party.

Instead of fighting tooth and nail for the proof of being right, by follow-ing verbal judo you refuse to make it a conversation about being right. When power struggles arise simply sidestepping them, as when a judo contestant is sparring with a much larger opponent, will go a long way. You can do this by the practicing the following techniques:

- Refocus the parents on what you can do to improve the situation as opposed to arguing.
- Try to not think in terms of proving yourself but on improving the situation at hand.
- When the person comes at you full of emotion do not mirror this emotion. Step away or step back.
- Avoid directly engaging in a power struggle with power and resistance.

BELIEF IS 110% REALITY

There used to be a show on television that was about how people winning large sums of money in the lottery had their lives ruined. Now, one may ask, how is that possible? If I won the lottery that would never be a problem for me; I would buy some tropical island somewhere, a sports car, and live hap-pily ever after. Yet, this was their reality; somehow what many would consider an amazing stroke of luck became a terrible fate.

This may be an extreme example, but we all go around with our own lenses of the world. For some of us they are rose-colored, tinted with only the most positive notions of everyone's intentions as well as our own. Others walk around with gray-tinted sunglasses, looking at the world with suspicion and negativity. The point is that all of us have our own reality that we hold tight to as tried and true.

To tell any parents that their beliefs or perceptions are wrong is like trying to tell someone that his or her blue shirt is not blue. People hold on to their realities, so do not try to push your reality upon them. Meet them where they are and then deal with it accordingly. Likewise, if you speak to parents and tell them they "should not feel the way they do," you are not respecting their reality. Also, telling them "I know how you feel because ...," even if you have been through a similar situation, does not help because you cannot understand their feelings in terms of their unique situation and reality. So, avoid making such a statement if possible.

THE "IDIOTS" AND "THE CRAZY FOOLS"

One of the best ways of understanding how we resolve and handle conflict is to analyze situations of extreme stress. For many, nothing provokes as much stress as that of driving on the highway. If you notice, when you drive along the highway, you will become angered at those "idiots" who drive too slowly for your liking as well as those "crazy people" who speed past you.

It will most likely never occur to you that your speed and driving ability plays into the equation. Also, you will not tend to consider that perhaps the person is driving slowly because his or her car is not functioning well or there is an accident up ahead. Concurrently, you would immediately judge the car that is going faster than you, but you do not know if perhaps there is an emergency to which the driver is responding by driving fast.

Do you notice as well that you do not criticize the drivers in a calm, passive, semijudgmental manner such as, "Boy they drive slowly." Rather, you go immediately for their jugular and attack them as individuals using terms like "idiot" or "crazy fool." This is what is known in conflict resolution and psychology as the fundamental attribution error (a term coined by social psychologist Lee Ross), which is defined as the tendency in times of conflict or stress to lean toward attacking the person versus the situation.[1]

Be cautious because this is an easy trap to fall into. It is far easier to go after the person than the situation because if the person is morally wrong or defective, you don't have to worry about correcting the situation at hand. Rather, the parents, the faculty members, or the students are the problem and so changing them in some way is the only viable solution.

PARENT ASSOCIATIONS AND PARENTAL CONFLICT

Parental organizations offer you an opportunity to test the climate of the bigger picture of your relationships with parents as a whole. If you are going to have a conflict, in terms of a global school issue, these parents may be the barometer that the storm is coming soon. Therefore, it is important to have a friendly relationship, while at the same time maintaining a healthy level of distrust and skepticism with parental associations.

Setting boundaries early with these parents is important. Each year a different set of members will join the executive boards of the various PTA/PTO groups and, therefore, you will (much like a teacher) have a PTA/PTO with a different attitude and dynamic. Still, remember that these parents, while well meaning, often do not know how involved they can become or what the expectations or the limits of their participation with the day-to-day operations and relationship with the larger school community are. It is up to you to forge this in an assertive yet nonaggressive manner early and proactively.

DON'T DILUTE YOUR STATEMENTS

Sometimes, we have a habit of using words like "ummmm,"… "like," "kind of," "you know," "we," etc. These utterances and words serve to fill space, while we think of the next statement we want to bridge into. The issue is that it takes away the power and emphasis of your perspective statement.

Additionally, these words/phrases make you seem uncertain of your point of view. They dilute what you are going to do or are about to say with an air of hesitation and uncertainty. It would be better to wait on your words and pause. In doing so, it allows you to be cautious and pensive and provides gravity to what you are trying to say.

FISHER AND URY'S "BANTA"

Roger Fisher, a law professor at Harvard University, and William Ury, another professor at the esteemed university, teamed together to create a group called the Harvard Negotiation Project. They authored several highly acclaimed books on the subject of conflict resolution including the international bestseller *Getting to Yes*.[2]

In this book they coined the term (which has now become a classical concept and phrase) BANTA—The Best Alternative to a Negotiated Agreement. That is, when you decide ahead of time the bottom line of what you will accept before you go into a conflict with a faculty member or a parent.

Why? Because now you have a foundation from which to work versus going in blindly with no basement or groundwork of what may be acceptable.

YOUR FIRST LINE OF DEFENSE

The first line of defense for educators is the secretaries. They are the heart and soul of a school. These are first people to greet the public and the ones who know the very pulse of the school. They could also be on the firing line for parent rants and complaints. If you are going to have an advertisement for your school, secretaries are the ones who are the neon signs that flash what your school is about. Be certain that the sign is bright and a good representative of the school versus one of those signs that loudly hums and has half of its letters burned out and dimmed. Remind them as well of the parental types that may "befriend" them and about security, gossip, and professionalism.

It is important to be certain that they are trained on how to handle, in a nonaggressive yet assertive manner, the parents coming into the door. It is also vital that they are given direction as to dividing parents into those that should be seen immediately, those that can be referred for a phone call, and those whose parental issues can wait. Advise them that you will need a "heads up" on potential issues as well as concerns; this will go a long way in preventing headaches in the years ahead. Most of all, be certain that they are friendly, yet assertive, and are chosen as seriously as any other staff member.

WHAT IS YOUR PARENTING STYLE?

We tend to judge others based on what we think is appropriate in terms of parenting. But, who's to say that your parenting is the best and most efficient means? We all operate on a spectrum of more permissive, rigid, or democratic parenting styles. How you tend to parent (when, and if, you eventually become a parent) will determine what you accept as typical, "good," or "appropriate" parenting and subsequently what you judge as not.

Therefore, be aware of your parenting style and that others may have diverse child-rearing styles to yours based on their upbringing, culture, finances, age, etc. Be aware that you have this attribution bias toward others and step back accordingly.

Appendix E includes a quick parenting survey and questionnaire that can give you a basic idea of what your parenting style is (or will be) and that can give you some insight into the style you predominantly utilize/will utilize in parenting.

STRIKE WHILE THE IRON IS COLD

When do we first call most parents? When we have an issue with a child. Therefore, the first conversation we have with parents is a negative one—your child is bad. Now, we tell them that their child's behavior was negative or that the child made a bad choice (take your pick of educational jargon). However, the first thing parents hear in their head is that you are criticizing their child, the fruit of their loins.

Fortunately, most children have a honeymoon period at the beginning of every school year in which they are testing the waters and boundaries. When a child enters through the doors of our school, we can learn a great deal based on alleged history and reputation of the pupil's past. This is the right time to contact the parents—before an issue heats up. This is the period to say something positive about their son/daughter. You may say, "Yes, but I don't have time to do that. Especially at the start of a school year." Well, if you do not do it then, you will be doing it throughout the year anyway.

Keep in mind, human nature is to remember the negative. If you think back to when you were in high school, it is a good chance that you remember the kids who were the "trouble makers" more than the honors students. If I were to ask you what the most negative thing said to you by your parents was, you would be more likely to recall that more quickly than the most positive thing your mother or father said to you.

In counseling circles there is an informal rule called the "One for Five Rule." Basically, it states that it takes five positive comments to equal the weight of one negative statement. Imagine if a family believes they have been saddled with a history of negative relationships within a school, what will that mean for all the comments that will have to be made to put the relationship in positive territory?

So, if you start off with a negative conversation, that will be how a parent remembers you. If you start off with a positive statement in those critical first "honeymoon days" you will be laying a firm foundation. Be behaviorally specific and seek to identify the positives in what you are saying, even if they are relatively minor.

Think that every time you say something positive you are adding equity into "the bank of parental trust." When you are saying something that the parent perceives as negative, you are making a withdrawal. Without enough money in your bank account with parents, the significant penalty for early withdrawal is usually a pervasive lack of trust.

EDUCATIONAL HISTORY—WHAT MAY NOT BE SAID TO YOU

Oftentimes when we consider the academic history of a student, we forget the parent's educational career. If a parent was classified as a child, it would have been vastly different from the current "least restrictive environment" paradigm we use today. Perhaps he or she has memories of being in a class segregated, bullied, as well as ostracized from the other students. Would you want this for your child?

Therefore, questioning not only what concerns they have for their child but also what their educational experience was like is a key to understanding the deep-rooted concerns parents may have for their children.

HOME LIFE—WHAT MIGHT NOT BE SHOWN TO YOU

Difficult parents and difficult lives often go hand in hand. Imagine having a home in which you are struggling to keep the lights on, the water running, and food on the table. It happens in the most impoverished and the most affluent districts. How do you prioritize?

As we stated earlier, if someone is drowning, the first thing that person will do is seek to get a breath of air. If you are the lifeguard going out to save that person, he or she may well pull you under in a desperate attempt to survive. Parents who are desperate to survive day to day and are looking for their next meal are not in a place where they can have a discussion about homework.

Look toward your school counselor to gain an understanding of the history of a family and join in their concerns as well as needs. Sometimes, the first things they need are the basics before they can even entertain a conversation on education.

AVOID ALPHABET SOUP

When you go to the doctor, if you ever read his or her notes or watched him or her speak to another physician, you can empathize with the "alphabet soup" of the medical world. Initials that you don't understand and words and phrases you may not recognize leave you hanging onto every word to understand how they are gauging your health.

Education is no different; IEP, BD, LLD, SLE, FBA—we have initials for everything. If you are having an "I&RS" (Intervention and Referral Services Meeting) no parent would want to meet with what they think is the "IRS." The point is, we talk with our colleagues using the language of educational professionals. When we do not translate this for parents, it does not allow them to feel comfortable and understand, from a noneducator's perspective, what is truly going on.

BE LIKE THE PAST TV JUDGES, NOT THE PRESENT

In the 1980s there was a TV court show that featured an older, stoic veteran judge. He never made a decision without "retiring to his chambers" to ponder first. No matter what the case, big or small, he would take the time to think about what his verdict was going to be. As a result, his decisions showed logic, rationality, and poise.

Flash forward twenty plus years later and watch any of the current court shows. Now, in the rapid pace of the post-Internet era, television judges don't take the time to deliberate. Rather, they shout, yell, cajole, and make judgments by the seat of their pants. As a result, they make hasty decisions that are heavily streaked emotionally, heavy handed or illogical, as well as high on entertainment value.

So, what can you learn from this? Use the former veteran judge's technique versus the latter. Do not be forced into making a choice. Do not use emotions to constitute and fabricate a nonexistent emergency that creates a hasty decision that is ill-conceived. Take a break, retreat alone "to your chamber" without making a forced decision, and come back with a well-balanced, smart, and logical verdict. Remember, if everything is an emergency, nothing becomes an emergency.

REMEMBER LOYALTY IS EVERYTHING

Parents will change as students cycle through your school. Faculty, however, lasts forever, at least metaphorically speaking. Therefore, if you must choose sides between a conflict with a parent and a faculty member, plan accordingly. Be careful when you side with a parent as this may have a lasting effect on the overall school climate and your level of trust among the faculty within the school is longer lasting.

- *Be certain that the "chain of command" is respected:* If possible, encourage going back and addressing the concerns with the teacher. If not, remember to attempt to solve the problem, and don't get pulled into the personal attacks against the teacher. If you avoid directly mentioning the teacher and bring the discussion back to the ultimate actions and goals the parent hopes to achieve, this will go a long way to prevent you from becoming entangled in an issue of crossing the bounds of your loyalties.
- *Avoid giving subtle hints (through body language, cues, or words) that you agree with the parents about their opinion of a lack of the educators teaching prowess:* Return as many times as needed to this issue. This is

about improving the student's learning aptitude, not criticizing the teacher's attitude.

- *Have the teacher present whenever possible:* If parents are going to discuss a teacher's performance, then the teacher should be there unless the parents specifically requests otherwise. If the teacher is not present, they will be left questioning how, and if, you defended them.
- *Avoid talking about any other faculty member in a negative fashion with any other staff (unless of course it is disciplinary in nature and necessary):* People will judge you inevitably more by what you do, not by what you say. If you are talking about someone, your staff will instinctively think that, since you are talking about a fellow faculty member negatively, it is only a matter of time before the negative spotlight is turned toward any one of them. ("If you talk to me about someone else ... you may talk about me.")
- *Write a quick note when you see a teacher going above and beyond:* If you see a teacher handle a situation with particular tact and aplomb, leave a quick note on his or her desk and be specific as to what you saw that you liked. Always keeping stationary at hand to do so will help maintain a positive climate. Faculty members who are applauded for positive behaviors are most likely to recreate those behaviors again and again.

LISTEN BEFORE TALKING

Oftentimes we are the first to talk when we meet with parents. We tell them the purpose of the meeting, how their child is doing in school, our impression of the child, etc., and then we carry on the meeting with a dialogue about potential solutions. Sometimes this meeting may be successful and positive, while at other times the conversation may go down a path that quickly spirals into a negative tornado of conflict and discord.

If we first ask the parents what their opinion of their child's education thus far is, in an open-ended way, we find points of agreement. For instance, if we start off meeting with parents by asking them how they see their child's school year going, we may learn that the parents are struggling to get their child do his or her homework, they are noticing their child having difficulty paying attention, etc. Now, we have a point of common agreement and dialogue. However, if we start talking first we miss these points or, worse yet, we talk over potential points of agreement. In doing so, we enter and violate areas of sensitivity without recognizing them and then become like a proverbial "bull in a China shop."

DON'T FIX WHAT CANNOT BE FIXED

As an educator you have probably heard horrific and devastating stories of what your students and families have undergone. From domestic violence, to poverty, to illness, the terrible situations that we bear witness to in our school communities can be overwhelming to the family and difficult for educators to not bring home on their backs at the end of the school day.

That being said, we are not in the respective parents' shoes. As educators we are all counselors and social workers in addition to teachers. If we did not care, we probably would have burned out and moved onto a less emotionally demanding profession within the first five years of our teaching career. (This time frame, according to National Public Radio, is when nearly half the number of educators transfer to a new school or leave education altogether.[3])

So what do we say when parents bring up these issues? Issues of despair, fear, anxiety, and sadness? Nothing, we just listen. If a parent really feels listened to, versus provided unsolicited advice of, "you know what I would do" they will feel at ease. This type of unsolicited advice may not be the answer(s) they need. When we tell parents how to fix issues that are not capable of being fixed, we come across as less empathetic and, worse yet, we give opinions that were not asked for. There is the saying, "If it ain't broke don't fix it." In our case, "If you can't fix it, just listen to it genuinely and kindly." Sometimes just being a shoulder to cry on is better than any advice you can offer.

AVOID SUBTLE JUDGMENT IN YOUR WORDS

In the *New York Times* bestselling book *Difficult Conversation* by the Harvard Negotiation Project's Douglas Stone, Bruce Patton, and Shelia Heen, the authors suggest being cautious with regard to interactions that you inadvertently deem as "truthful" within your interactions.[4]

This means that words that are token in our field—such as "appropriate," "inappropriate," "wrong/right," or "professional"—have judgment embedded in them. How? Who are you to tell a parent what is appropriate, inappropriate, what is right and wrong, or what is a professional? In each of these we are placing concrete statements as to what is the "correct" or "incorrect" way of doing things. This is, perhaps, irrelevant to the parent's belief system, culture, or opinion.

Therefore, it is important that when you do make such a statement with regard to these issues, you make it known that this is your opinion versus fact. The authors of *Difficult Conversations* make an excellent point that it is not that your comment has no truth (or to what degree you are truthful);[5]

rather, it is just that it is important to distinguish the chasm between what is "opinion" and what you believe to be "fact."

LOUDER IS NOT ALWAYS BETTER

When a parent gets loud, don't mirror this volume. There is a tendency to raise your volume to get your point across. Lowering your voice can create the exact same effect more appropriately and effectively than being brash.

AVOID SARCASM

Oftentimes, we use sarcasm without even knowing it. Sometimes we utilize this technique to indirectly put forward a point, sometimes for humor, and other times for a bit of both.

The difficulty is that sarcasm is indirect and clouded communication. So, in an already muddied conflict in which you are trying to figure each other out, the sarcasm makes things even more difficult to comprehend. This means that one runs the very real risk of sarcasm taken as hostility (even when it is not intended). The best means of avoiding this trap is to simply avoid sarcasm when engaging with a parent or a faculty member in a high-tension discussion.

This is also a prime reason to avoid texts, e-mails, or social media messages related to work. People who cannot read into the message can falsely take communication negatively or as sarcasm.

NOTES

* "Whenever You're in Conflict with Someone, There Is One Factor That Can Make the Difference between Damaging Your Relationship and Deepening It. The Factor Is ATTITUDE." Positively Positive. Accessed April 10, 2016. http://www.positivelypositive.com/quotes/the-factor-is-attitude

1. Ito, Mamie. "Fundamental Attribution Schema." *PsycEXTRA Dataset.* doi:10.1037/e342482004-001.

2. Fisher, Roger, and William Ury. *Getting to Yes: Negotiating Agreement without Giving in.* New York, NY: Penguin, 2011, 99–108

3. "The Teacher Dropout Crisis." NPR. Accessed April 08, 2016. http://www.npr.org/sections/ed/2014/07/18/332343240/the-teacher-dropout-crisis.

4. Stone, Douglas, Bruce Patton, and Sheila Heen. *Difficult Conversations: How to Discuss What Matters Most.* New York, NY: Viking, 1999.

5. Novick, Brett "15 Ways to Involve 'At Risk' Parents" In Enrichment Programs, NJEA Review, December 2014.

Chapter 5

A Deeper Dive

Looking under the Surface

We always see the point of an iceberg. So I've always accepted the idea that people—they don't necessarily know everything I am.

—Olivier Theyskens*

CULTURE

No conversation about any kind of human interaction would be possible without a reminder of how culture impacts our ability to understand parental relationships and how these belief systems affect the paradigm lens of how families interact on a daily basis.

For instance, when working with an Orthodox family it may be inappropriate for a woman to be touched in any way by a male who is not her husband. If you are a man and have extended your hand for a simple handshake you may have caused offense literally before saying anything.

The best means of becoming culturally competent is to ask questions. Read about the cultures that are predominant in your school and experience them by immersing yourself as best as possible. Traveling, trying a new ethnic restaurant, learning new languages, or befriending a wide diversity of friends, all help in this comprehension skill.

Similarly, the following are but a very condensed and nonexhaustive list of cultural etiquette:

• *Remember that cultural differences do not mean that all persons act the same way in any particular culture. Generalizations can lead to biases, which can be offensive.*

- *If you are making small talk, avoid any topics that could be inflammatory or inadvertently offensive. These would include things such as: humor, politics, and religion.*
- *Personal space tends to be a preference according to culture. In North America we tend to take more of a distance when it comes to personal space whereas in many Latin America cultures people tend to be closer talkers.*
- *Some South American countries consider direct eye contact to be rude or offensive. This is important to know because in the United States we tend to consider those who do not make eye contact deceitful.*
- *Persons who are of the Muslim or Orthodox Jewish religions forbid any physical contact with the opposite sex.*
- *People in the United States tend to consider a firm, crisp handshake the sign of a confident and strong person. Asian cultures tend to find this aggressive and prefer a head nod, bow, or light handshake. Additionally, Asian cultures tend to prefer less constant eye contact.*
- *Even in various places within the United States you will find varying levels of comfort and pace. In the Northeast, pace tends to be faster than in the Midwest or in the West. In the Midwest, people tend to speak slower and may take more time with small talk versus getting to the heart of a conversation. Likewise, northeasterners may tend to use more physical contact in their interactions.*
- *If you are not certain of whether something is offensive, ask questions. It may seem like common sense; however, common sense is not always common among all faculty members.*
- *Be aware of calendar(s) and holidays outside of the traditional secular holidays that may impact a student or family during the school year and have a basic understanding of these as such. A good idea is to look at your local department of education's list of holidays for which students may be excused from school.*

It may not be all-inclusive, however, you can get familiarized with the range of cultures and understand why students may be absent on certain days or for certain lengths of time. In the state of New Jersey, for instance, there are more than 100 holidays that a student may be excused from school for.[1]

- *Remember that families constitute a very diverse swath of people. Families consist of traditional nuclear families, foster families, guardians, same-sex families, and single-parent families. This means that we must be careful to adapt our communications in each manner to all that the word "family" encompasses.*
- *Many workshops are available on cultural awareness/sensitivity, both online and traditionally. These can provide invaluable assistance in this area.*

- *If you are meeting with members of a family who are not English-language speakers, have a translator available, even if they seem fairly proficient in English, just in case.*
- *Smiling and kindness crosses all cultures and language barriers. So do food, family, and friends—we all have these in common.*[2]

PLAN AHEAD FOR MEETINGS

Sometimes there may be a need for an "emergency meeting" to address issues of safety or welfare of a student in school. The vast majority of the time, however, our gatherings are planned and intentional. Yet, many times consultations can degrade to going over the same issue(s) over and over again and become stuck on a treadmill of inaction, wasting the time of all involved. This cycle leads to high frustration, emotion, and nothing productive.

Before a meeting is established, we should have an agenda of what we hope to accomplish. Sounds simple enough, right? Well how many times have you been to a meeting in which you knew the mission of what needed to be accomplished? Be certain that everyone knows what is hoping to be accomplished.

Sometimes as an administrator you will get a phone call that a parent wants to come in for a meeting. You may have no idea why, what is needed, or even who should be involved. This sets the precedent for a very frustrating and unproductive meeting to come. Parents have the right to request a meeting, but they also need to be reminded that in order for you to be productive in a meeting certain ground rules need to be on the table: a basic reason for a meeting and a framework of what they hope to accomplish by it. Only then, can you truly have an opportunity to prepare for a meeting.

When you are at a meeting, look at where everyone sits. Why? Because you can tell a great deal from the sitting arrangement. Are the mother and father sitting apart? Is it staff on one side and parent(s) on the other? If you see the former arrangement this may be a sign of emotional distance or parental disagreement with each other. If it is parents on one side, faculty on the other, the best way to deal with this is to place yourself immediately next to the parents. In doing so, you are saying nonverbally "I am in this with you together." This simple act, may serve to provide reassurance as well as decrease hostility.

Those who have a knack for saying the wrong thing dwell among every faculty. These are people whose mouths, when open, smell like shoe leather from their inserting their foot in it too many times. When we have a meeting we should know (for the most part) who is going to say what. We should also, more importantly, know who shouldn't say what and avoid anyone (or everyone) saying the same thing more than once. There is nothing more frustrating and disheartening in a meeting than each educator saying the same thing in different ways to the family because we all feel we have to participate in the conversation.

Let's take an example from a marriage and family counseling session that illustrates this point well. During that session the husband decides to "unload" on his wife that he had been unfaithful to her for several months and was going to divorce her. There is silence when he says this—an uncomfortable deafening quiet. The novice counselor squirms in his chair and then, to fill the vacuum, he asks, "How does that make you feel?" The wife returns a cold, steely glare and says, "How do you think it makes me feel?"

Later, the counseling supervisor turns to the rookie therapist when they leave and says, "What was the clinical significance of asking that? Were you doing that for a clinical purpose or because you were uncomfortable with silence?" The freshly minted therapist was uncomfortable and so is desperate to break the quiet with something—anything. The point clearly illustrates if you have nothing that is going to add to the conversation that is different or useful, avoid it.

Often meetings go smoothly and we leave relieved that it did not turn into a hostile parental interaction. Conversely, sometimes we are "blindsided" by seemingly innocuous meetings that go terribly wrong. If possible, when we are meeting with parents, having a general plan as to what we must do should things go south is very useful. Training the faculty to be proactive in how we deal with meetings should they begin to go badly is always beneficial. Just as we plan for fire drills and varying crisis drills, we should also plan for potential problematic meetings. This will also help prevent faculty members making "false promises" of things that may be offered to parents, which cannot be fulfilled due to the fear of climaxing conflict.

Meetings are not meant to go on forever. After a certain point, anything positive that is going to be gleaned from a meeting has probably already taken place, and a backslide to a lack of productivity and negative communication starts to occur. Therefore, a definitive time frame should be established prior to meeting. If you do not do so, you risk a negative interaction with a parent, and if you have others waiting to meet you have already established a potential point of irritation for all subsequent conferences going forward now that you have caused a domino effect of late parental get-togethers for the rest of the day.

So how do you do so in a fashion that is not rude? First, let the family know the amount of time that you have slated for the meeting. Next, be sure that you have the family sitting with their back to the clock so you can glance over their shoulder subtly to see the time instead of looking at your watch or making it obvious you are checking the time. When you are ready to finish the meeting, tell them that you wish to understand all that took place prior to ending the meeting and review what was discussed so they know that they, and their concerns, were listened to. A printed out copy of points discussed may even be provided if this is your preference.

Be aware that some families, when you wish to conclude a conference/meeting may "drop a bomb." That is, they will bring up an important topic at the conclusion of your time together to give fresh fuel to carry your interactions to some indefinite point. To this end, assure them that you have heard this concern and will reschedule to discuss this issue at an upcoming date.

There is a very real tendency to "take the bait," so to speak, of a parent giving you some tasty morsel of information at the waning minutes of a meeting. Avoid it at all costs, as this provides the parents an opportunity to step over the boundary of a slated meeting time and thus continue the meeting at the peril of all those parents waiting and staff held hostage to doing other necessary duties that are also slated for that day. Of course, if anyone discusses safety issues this is the one glaring and important exception (as these issues must always be addressed quickly and expediently).

LOOK FOR WHAT IS NOT BEING SAID

When you have a parental meeting, sit back for a minute. Take in "what is not being said," that is, the nonverbal cues of the room. Who is sitting with who? What is the body language of each member of the room? Who is joking? Who is serious?

By doing this you will have a leg up on those others who just trudged into the room, simply looking for what will be said. Dr. Albert Mehrabian, author of *Silent Messages*, discovered that a full 55% of communication is found through nonverbal means.[3] Imagine the advantage you will have if you can take in just a portion of this communication in a meeting.

Additionally, as noted previously, you can help cause a parent to be less anxious or less potentially angered by simply sitting next to him or her. How many times do you see all the staff stacked at one side of the room and then the lonely parent left to fend for himself or herself at the head of the table?

Sitting next to that parent will provide some very real comfort that you are on their side. It also is very difficult for a parent to glare angrily at you when you are shoulder to shoulder discussing his or her child. This one subtle case seems less threatening in nature than glaring at another from across a table.

DID YOU NAME ONE STRENGTH FOR EVERY ONE ISSUE?

Oftentimes, when we have a meeting, we look to find problems. After all, isn't the goal of a meeting to solve problems?

The difficulty is when we seek to improve on a student, behaviorally or academically, we pinpoint certain issues. This, in turn, skews our perspective toward problem finding and solving. In doing so, we lose also perspective toward a balanced view.

Therefore, look for strengths to provide a more balanced and fair view of the student to the parent. This should be done prior to the meeting and should be the first thing brought up so as to avoid forgetting it during the meeting/conversation with the parent.

WHAT DOES A CLASSIFICATION OR DIAGNOSIS MEAN?

Sometimes in a challenging meeting or conversation with a family we are seeking to find the classification or diagnosis of a student. Are they autistic? Do they have attention deficit hyperactivity disorder (ADHD)? Are they learning disabled? We go around in circles and expend a vast amount of energy pondering this.

While these are great questions, they can steer a meeting toward ineffectiveness. Why? Because, first off, if we don't have enough information or if we are not qualified to do the diagnosis or classification at that time what is the use of that discussion at that specific time? Secondly, and more importantly, a diagnosis or classification does not tell us what to do once we have it.

For instance, suppose you go to the doctor and he or she tells you that you have a disease that you have not heard of; the first question is what is it, but the next, more important, question is how do we treat it. This being said, the most important concern once you give a student a label in the form of a classification/diagnosis is "Now what?" What you do to address the issue (diagnoses, classified or not) is vastly more important and productive than anything else.

EYEING UP THE "I" MESSAGES

Perhaps the most stressful and difficult conflicts to resolve are those of spouses. Couples are highly charged, and getting in between the two can be like sticking a screwdriver in a light socket without shutting the fuse. Fortunately, there is a technique that is the hallmark of couples' counseling that is so simple you can use it in any challenging conversation with parents—the "I" message.

The "I" Message simply starts off with using the word "I" when you are indicating your opinion. Use of the word "I" keeps you from pointing a verbal finger at somebody or trying to seemingly escape responsibility. Next, follows the statement on how you feel about a situation and it is done clearly without overly sugar coating the message. Finally, a potential solution of what you need for hopeful resolution of the problem is done in a behaviorally specific and objective manner.

This method, though simple, avoids verbally attacking a person. It also keeps the other party from feeling unduly blamed for the cause, as well as verbalizes a clear potential solution for the issue at hand. Remember, when you point a finger metaphorically at others, three are pointed directly back at you.

EMOTIONALITY AND RATIONALITY ARE LIKE OIL AND WATER

If you would, let's go back to the lifeguard analogy used earlier. The first thing they teach you when you make a rescue is to be aware that when you swim out to a person who is drowning, he or she will try to grab you and pull you under. It is not that the victim intends on endangering you, logic would tell the drowning person to relax and let you (the lifeguard) bring him or her to land safely. Emotions, however, tell this person that this is the only and last desperate hope of getting in a few additional frantic breaths before drowning. In other words, emotionality and rationality are like trying to mix oil and water.

Parents can behave in much the same way when meeting with educators. Remember, rationality and emotionality are two very separate things. If you want to speak to parents rationally listen to them emotionally first. Don't think that when you have overly emotional parents that you can somehow rationalize them into being rational.

If they are emotional, they are the opposite of rational so that emotional void needs to be filled. You can then move onto the next and more productive job of dealing with a transitional as well as rational framework.

"IS IT WORTH THE BATTLE?"

Ask yourself that question before you engage in a difficult conversation with a parent. Question yourself:

1. Will this provide some appreciable help for the student currently or in the near future?
2. Is this an issue that directly affects the students', peers', or faculty members' safety?
3. Is this on the "top three" list of issues I would want to address with this parent?
4. Looking at the history with this parent, will it make any appreciable difference or is it better to handle this issue internally within the parameters of what we can do within the school?
5. Is this the right time to deal with this? Some issues need to be dealt with immediately while others should be examined to find patterns or to see further how they are playing out.
6. Is this an issue that is simply a "pet peeve" of mine but in the larger scheme of things is a microcosm of what I should be dealing with in regard to this student or the class as a whole?

ANGER: THE ULTIMATE ICEBERG

When you look at an iceberg you see a majestic mountain of ice that juts far into the air. Looking at that splendor it is hard to imagine that an even more enormous structure lies several feet under the water at the base of that very iceberg.

Anger is an emotion that is very much the same. When you see anger in parents, there is a tendency to attack back with further aggression. This quickly erupts into a power struggle with all the success of two sumo wrestlers smacking their large bodies against each other for supremacy.

Look beyond the anger, dive deeper, and see what you find? Angry parents are also parents who are concurrently likely frustrated, fearful, or worried for their child. You have told them that something is wrong with their flesh and blood and they instinctively are responding like a bear trying to protect its cub.

What if you said, "I see you seem worried for your child ... can you tell us about how we can help with that?" "This must be frustrating for you as well after you told us he refuses to do his homework for you ... what is that like?" When you explore these feelings you are going under that anger and making an emotional connection that often serves to decrease or eliminate the aggression.

Also, remember that anger has two components: the brain-based and the body-based. If parent seem as though they are not angered they may still have residual, physical feelings of anger. Therefore, allow some time for their water to proverbially stop boiling by taking a short break if you notice the meeting becoming too white hot with anger.

MORE ON POWER STRUGGLES

We often do not realize it, but by our role we are at the advantage in terms of power with the parents when we are in the school setting.

We have our educator peers, we are the administrators and educators, and the meeting is on our home turf. If a parent had a bad experience with a teacher, or remembers going to the principal as a child, these feelings come flowing back.

Why is this important? It is vital because we need to realize that just as the scales tipped in our favor in a meeting or interaction with these parents, it has created anxiety for them and we must do all we can to at least help eliminate the belief that they are at that disadvantage.

AVOID JUDGING

When you are in a meeting, some parents hang on your every word. What are they saying about my child? What aren't they saying? Why did they phrase it that way?

Therefore, be careful what you say and how you say it. If you are going to talk about a student's behavior, be specific. Don't label a child as "he is a problem child" or "none of his peers like him." Labels are for jars not students—one size does not fit all.

Instead of using judgmental terms with a student, be specific. So, when a student is one that has "chronic absenteeism," rather than telling the parents that their child is chronically absent, use numbers and statistics: "Joey has been out 34 of 100 days of school." This prevents parents from feeling like you are casting a judgment of them or their child, which creates hostility. It is easy to judge; but it does not foster much-needed change.

ABSOLUTELY NO ABSOLUTES

When conversing with parents in a difficult conversation avoid "black and white" sentences. In other words, if you use the words "always, never" you are indicating that there is never (ever) an exception to the problematic behavior.

Rather, discuss that their child on "most days" exhibits (whatever specific behavior you are seeing). It is more accurate and can then be tempered with when you have seen some semblance of good and appropriate behaviors as well as the balance between the two.

GRUDGES, POLITICS, AND ALL THAT

It is very easy to hold grudges against those who have wronged you, whether parent, faculty member, or even student. As a former coworker used to sing to the tone of the Christmas song "Let it snow ... let it snow ... let it snow ... let it go ... let it go ... let it go!"

Getting involved in grudges is easy in any field in which you are working directly with so many people. The difficulty is that when you hold grudges it makes you seem petty and you begin to lose the respect of others, aside from the person you hold a grudge against. Likewise, you damage relationships that later may not be able to be fully repaired when you may need them for a specific purpose. A quote from Buddha surmises this best, "Holding on to anger is like drinking poison and expecting the other person to die."

Every workplace has politics; none may be more wrought with politics than the world of a public school. One must understand that politics is a very real entity that exists in every system in which there are people. Cliques, favoritism, and even backstabbing can occur just under a seemingly civilized surface. Politics is a game that some choose to play to varying degrees. If you have a strong set of values and principles, however, you can quickly realize that as the spot on the horizon upon which you make your decisions and the yoke that keeps your ethical compass steady. If you are lacking this moral navigation you will quickly be swept into the bob and flow of the waves of politics that will allow you to blur your morals for one or two discretions and then lead down a destructive and dangerous path of administrative blindness.

No matter how large a district you are in, you will find there is always a lot less than seven degrees of separation, so don't burn bridges if you can help it. As Ralph Ellison stated most eloquently, "Education is all a matter of building bridges." Another quote by an unknown author warns of doing so stating, "Careful not to burn bridges, you just might need to cross back."

DOCUMENT, DOCUMENT, DOCUMENT

If you have a student who has been exhibiting negative behaviors in class, he or she will tend to drain you of all of your energy and emotions. Educators often wait for the next roller coaster ride of emotion or oppositional behavior white-knuckled and afraid of what each class or day may bring.

When you notice negative behaviors, document them, make a note of when they occur, and what they look like. It may seem like common sense, but when you are in the midst of behavioral issues within a classroom setting you tend to forget these important elements.

So how does this relate with parental interactions? If you are able to provide factual information to parents, it bridges to a more rational versus emotional conversation with them. Additionally, you may be able to find a pattern of behaviors that you can share with the parents. This makes you look like a willing partner, helping them solve the concerns of their child's behavior together, as you may be able to relate to them a missing piece of information that they failed to notice in their child while at home.

PREPARE FOR THE MEETING

How many times have you been in a meeting that falls apart? It starts off with good intentions; everyone wants to be productive and work through the issue. The parents, the administrator, the teacher are all involved and open for change. Yet, as the gathering drags on (and on and on) it degenerates into a nonstop treadmill of rehashing the same issues over and over again.

The meeting then ends (much later than intended) and everyone leaves exhausted as they realize they are back where they started. It lends itself to a frustrating experience for educator and parent alike. Everyone leaves scratching their heads as to what happened (or didn't happen) during that meeting that stretched on for hours.

Before a meeting, it is vital that we ask ourselves the following questions to ensure that the meeting is effective and efficient and does not become an exercise in frustration and futility.

WHAT ARE YOU HOPING TO ACCOMPLISH IN THIS MEETING?

Be as specific as possible. The more specific you are the more you can see if you are heading in the right direction and make correctional adjustments as needed.

1. *Who is going to sit where?*
2. As mentioned earlier, avoid the "us versus them" setup in which educational staff are on one side of the table and parents are on the other.

WHO IS GOING TO TELL THE PARENT/FAMILY
WHAT PARTICULAR INFORMATION?

We all have some faculty members (including ourselves) who do not mix well with certain parents. Then we have other staff members who have such a bad case of "insert foot into mouth disease" that their breath should perpetually smell like leather.

Find the best person to deliver the message to the parent, and others should be told when it may be best to keep silent.

If you are the one who should be silent, accept this. Again, we all have different parental types we mix better with. If you are not the best one for this particular mix of parents, stay quiet and unoffended.

WHAT HAPPENS SHOULD THINGS GO WRONG?

Many times sessions go well. Everyone stays civil and although not productive they are also not harmful to the relationship between the parent and the school.

Sometimes, however, meetings quickly degenerate into a screaming match or a situation where it is clear that the interactions may be seriously detrimental to the relationship between a faculty member and a parent.

To avoid this, have an emergency plan. If things are going badly, when do we stop the meeting? Who is going to be responsible for bringing the meeting back on track? How do we exit this meeting gracefully? We have all kinds of drills in school and a bad meeting drill may be a quick rehearsal to go through as well to avoid an issue in a meeting from raging into a full-blown wildfire.

HOW LONG IS THE TIME TOGETHER GOING TO BE?

Many times we have a loose idea of when we want to end a meeting and then it drags on for much longer. The question then becomes how long is this meeting going to be? If we know this, we can designate a person to begin to wrap up the meeting in a manner that does not seem overly short or rude.

HOW ARE WE GOING TO CLOSE THE GATHERING?

As mentioned in the above point, closure of a meeting is crucial. One of the best ways to do this is to conduct a review of the meeting in which all concerns are readdressed to make certain the parents know that their concerns have been heard, documented, and understood. Again though, whoever is best at handling this particular family should be the one who terminates and concludes the consultation.

WHAT ARE YOU ABLE TO PROVIDE AND PROMISE TO THE FAMILY, AND WHAT CAN'T YOU PROVIDE?

In a world that is chock-full of all types of educational laws, we must tread lightly when making promises in a meeting. Promises (intended or implied) can have real potential legal consequences and yet we often don't talk about what options we can provide before a meeting.

Be certain that all educators in a meeting should know prior to a meeting what they can provide in terms of services to a family and what are "off the table" and are not going to be possible to give. There is little else that causes more of a wrench in a meeting with a family than when someone with loose lips suggests that something can be provided for them that is then shot down as not possible.

Such a statement shows parents that school personnel have something that they can provide their child, but they are choosing to not to do so. It does not matter if it is possible to provide that service or not; now the parent thinks that the faculty are being deceitful and shady in terms of what they can, and will, offer.

IS WHAT YOU ARE SAYING WITHIN THE PARAMETER OF BOARD POLICY AND LAW?

I know, this seems like the most common sense statement. However, in the frenetic and ever-changing world of education, special education law, and board policy, and because of some who say what is on their mind and promise the world without thinking of potential consequence, one must always, unfortunately, be proactive to counter this.

WHO IS GOING TO DOCUMENT THE MEETING?

When you start a meeting with a parent, be certain, if it's not you, that someone is documenting the proceedings. It goes without saying that someone who is detail oriented and has legible handwriting or good computer skills should be chosen for this task.

ARE THERE TOO MANY CHEFS RUINING THE SAUCE?

Try to limit the meeting participants to those that are absolutely vital to be present. The more persons you have in a meeting, theoretically, the less effective the meeting will be. Why? Because as everyone has their say in the meeting it often creates more complexity and is more likely that the agenda will deviate off topic. Therefore, in this case, less is often more when it comes to being effective and efficient.

GIVE THE FAMILY A TRANSLATOR

I don't mean a language translator (although that is occasionally necessary). Give them a sheet that explains briefly in plain English abbreviations, acronyms, and terms that could be used in an educational meeting. Better yet, put the list on the website.

THE "LEAKY PIPE" THEORY

Imagine if you were a plumber and were called to a home for a water leak. You get to the call and notice a large crack in a pipe. You have a few options: patch it, replace it, or reroute the water from the pipe.

Likely (and hopefully) not on your shortlist of possibilities would be the option to put more water in the very pipe that caused the leak. Yet, we follow the same logic (or lack thereof) when we constantly call to involve an uninvolved parent and do not get an adequate response. How many times do you call a parent about a student with chronic behavioral issues only to have the parent not respond or give empty promises of support? Or, just as frustrating, trying several numbers none of which are in service?

Now, after a while you must ask yourself who the slow learner is. If the parents are not responding to your request to help in supporting your behavioral interventions for their child in school, they are telling you a lot by doing nothing. They are saying tacitly, "When my child is in your school it is your problem. I am at work, at home, or somewhere else so don't bother me ... I am not going to respond."

We can continuously complain about the leak in parenting support and keep pouring our energies down the proverbial "leaky pipe," or we can develop internal school strategies, rewards, and motivations to support the child. Now, understand, that means you still must make phone calls and serve disciplinary actions for purposes of policy and documentation. It also means, however, that you are not going to expect to have a partner in the parental support realm.

E-MAIL ... YOUR BEST FRIEND OR WORST ENEMY

In our technologically fast-paced world, texting, tweeting, and e-mailing have replaced face-to-face communications. This can be great in that messaging is quick, efficient, and offers a concrete documentation of your correspondence.

The flip side is (exactly the problem) that e-mail and digital communications are quick, efficient, and offer documentation of your correspondence. This means that anything you say on the Internet can be brought back to haunt you. In a single quick e-mail to a challenging parent, you may have documented yourself into an issue.

If you are dealing with challenging or difficult parent, by nature they will take any communication you have with them in a negative or distorted manner. So, when you send them an e-mail you have a dual form of documentation. The parent can print out anything you have said and have written proof of something that you may have never intended to communicate.

Additionally, people can alter e-mails quite easily, change headings, take sentences or words out, etc. Now one might ask why someone would go to such lengths, as this seems overly paranoid. True as this may be, I am only allowing you to see another realm of possibility in the world of e-mail exchange.

However, if you contact a parent on the phone, you have a one-way form of documentation. This means that you will record what your conversation was in the way you intended it, while the parent does not have a form of computer-based messaging that could potentially trap you.

The use of a Microsoft Excel spreadsheet or similar program will allow you to take advantage of technology to jot down dates, times, who, and when you met or spoke with a parent. This will allow you to file away all your interactions with parents in a manner that you can easily recall two days or two years from now without having to carry around or file through hundreds of pages of documentation should an issue from the past crop up and have to be readdressed.

AVOID THE PARENTAL TRIANGLE

In family therapy circles there is a theory called "triangulation." Wikipedia defines triangulation "as a situation in which one family member will not communicate directly with another family member, but will communicate with a third family member, which can lead to the third family member becoming part of the triangle."[4] Triangulation, however, is not isolated to families, it can easily be applied to any kind of system including that of a public school.

This happens with parents as well, when they try to triangulate you into an issue with a teacher, fellow administrator, or another parent. They talk about that person, who is out of the proverbial loop, hoping that when they bend your ear they will get some sympathy or a willing ally to help them. These are parents who may attempt to trample limits by going to another source when they "triangulate" you into a conflict to balance things to their side.

These are parents who don't know or want to respect borders. With knowledge of this, it is best to stay out of being pulled into the Bermuda Triangle of parental conflict. In other words, be sure to instruct problem parents to the chain of command and talk to the teacher before moving up the ladder. It may not be that they are trying to be disrespectful; it may just be a lack of awareness of appropriate limits and how to navigate the educational system in a correct fashion.

THE 24-HOUR RULE

Even the best of us can have a day where we fly off the cuff. Unfortunately, when dealing with challenging families, you are often brought to an emotional brink on any given difficult day. So, when you receive a call from a parent who has called you fifteen times today or has had a tendency to push your buttons, be aware that you cannot take back what you say once it gets out. It's better to give yourself a day before contacting the parent when you are fresh and calm versus making a ten-minute angry call that you will regret the consequences of for weeks. As Abraham Lincoln once exclaimed, "Better to remain silent and be thought a fool than to speak and remove all doubt."

This does come with a good deal of risk, however, because if you wait too long or too often it would seem like you are procrastinating and avoiding contact all together, thus, indicating to the parents that you are either uncooperative or an administrator who does not find their phone calls important. This will lead to the parent skipping further contact with you and going up to the next member on the chain of command.

PUTTING YOUR HEAD IN THE SAND

Be cautious. Taking time to deescalate your anger is not the same thing as procrastinating. If you stick your head in the proverbial sand of procrastination when dealing with parents, it can have dire consequences.

Before you delay responding to a parent ask yourself the following questions:

- What is the history of these parents? Do they have a history of contacting those above you?
- Is this an emergency/safety issue?
- Has this gone through a chain of command and does the "buck" stop with you?
- If I don't answer this today will it be something that stays on my mind all night?
- Does my anger or frustration and the consequences that a conversation may cause now trump the risks of delaying this conversation?

If you answer yes to any of these questions, you likely do not have the luxury of a 24-hour rule. The issue is one that you must address immediately and so, if you are prone to anger outbursts, rehearse your script before you call, and then get it over with.

STEAM FROM THE EARS = NOTHING IN THE HEAD

When challenging talks occur with parents, they sometime dissolve into an angry, ranting parent. Not only is this uncomfortable but it is nonproductive because the parent is screaming. Put another way, if steam is coming out of the ears, nothing you say is likely going into the brain.

It's better to call off the meeting for a period of time that allows the dust and the snow globe of swirling hostility to settle in the parents' brain before hoping for productive communication.

If you have a parent who has a history of chronic anger or potential aggression, it is foreseeable to include a resource officer or security officer within earshot. This provides a subtle message that you are not going to tolerate a screaming match (or anything even more volatile).

PRETEND YOU DON'T UNDERSTAND

When you go to the doctor and see him or her talking about your case with another medical professional, how does it make you feel? They talk about CBCs, EKGs, EEGs and use words that, unless you are familiar, seem like a totally foreign language. This puts most of us in an uneasy state as we hang on every word striving to comprehend exactly what the doctors are saying.

We do the same thing in education, though. We throw around educational abbreviations like some language we are fluent in, and we may only give a brief translation of what we are talking about with parents. Oftentimes they agree or don't question us as they are afraid of appearing ignorant of the educational lingo.

If you are in a meeting with a parent, pretend you have absolutely no idea of anything about education and this is the first time you stepped into a school. Now, when an unfamiliar term comes up ask, "Do you understand that? Can you explain that term more clearly?" By doing this, you are giving this family what they may need—by your acting as an advocate to translate educational jargon to English.

CAN YOU PUT YOUR HEAD ON THE PILLOW AT NIGHT?

No one has to tell you education is a difficult and emotionally draining job. Often you are asked to mediate among some of the most challenging situations and have to be quick on your feet to make the right choices in issues that sometimes have a lot of gray areas to them.

One of the easiest and simplest tests is asking yourself whether you can you put your head on your pillow at night. If your decision to come out in a court of law or you were to have to describe it to your family would you (and they) be proud of you? Can you answer in the affirmative to the following questions?

- *Did I make the best decision with what information I had?*
- *Is this decision aligned with my values and mission educationally?*
- *Did I take the easy way out or the best way in?*
- *Does the outcome of this situation comply with our ethics, policies, and law?*
- *Is this decision the best for the student (or for the majority of students)?*
- *Did I ensure all safety issues were met first?*
- *Would I do it again?*
- *Do the positives outweigh the negatives?*
- *Can I put my head on the pillow at night knowing I did my very best and have no regrets or guilt?*

WHERE ARE YOU GOING?

Difficult interactions are all about give and take. They test what your values and your bounds are. How far can you push and be pushed? What are you willing to give up and what are the areas that you will hold tight to? If you do not know yourself and your goals, this will be all but impossible. Therefore, ask yourself the following vital questions before you step foot in the field of tackling a challenging conversation or scenario:

- *What are the values I wish to portray?* Whatever the values that you hold important to your character, then you must remain steadfast to them as they are the important guideposts that you will not cross nor allow parents to cross. For instance, safety is of overriding importance in any situation so if a family attempts to cross this line you will always give significant pushback.
- *What is your mission statement and your school's?* A mission statement is quite simply what your overarching goals are. It should be simple, objective, and possible. This is a statement you return to in each of your interactions with others.
- *What are the laws and policies and procedures?* Laws, policies, procedures, and codes of ethics precede anything that you may develop. These are the important structural framework that you should build your values, mission statement, and school environment around primarily.

COFFEE OR TEA WITH ME

Sometimes having a parent see the educators in a light that is not as threatening will build a relationship of trust. At the beginning of a school year (and periodically through each semester) having a cup of coffee/tea will allow you to slate time to converse with parents before a challenging issue comes up.

It also extends your reputation as someone who is approachable and willing to hear parents out. A word of caution, however, this can become an opportunity for parents to cross over boundary lines, as this type of event can seem to blur boundaries. Professionalism must be tempered with approachability.

FOLLOW UP ... FOLLOW UP ... FOLLOW UP

After you have a challenging conversation with a parent, chances are the issues are not going to be resolved then and there. There are going to be loose ends that need to be tied up. Be certain that you extend the courtesy of a follow-up phone call. Even if things seem to be resolved, attempt a follow-up.

You may say that you simply don't have the time for this. However, if you are in a different conversation with trying parents, the few minutes of engagement that you have with them on the front end will save you a lot of time dealing with the heartache of an escalating conflict on the back end when they feel that you have not heard them or completely dealt with the issue at hand.

LOOK FOR YOUR ACHILLES' HEEL

Many (most) of us have an issue (or more likely issues) that are particularly sensitive to us. In our lives we have a personal history that we try not to merge into our professional history. We all have matters of failure, hurt, or other issues that we have grappled which make us able to empathize with the students and families we work with.

It is important to know that these are for you. These are the concerns that will break through your professional armor and may impact you personally or cause you to have an emotional reaction that may seem out of context or character. This is just a word of caution, to understand yourself your history and to know how others' life stories will impact your own.

AVOID RUDENESS

Sometimes we forget common courtesies when having a conversation with a family that can lead them down a bumpy road of being turned off. This is especially true if we are trying to make a first impression that we only get one shot at.

Here are some examples of what families may consider rude behavior:

- *Typing away at the computer while they are speaking:* The clatter of keyboards is distracting. Of further issue is, as you peer up from the keyboard and make limited eye contact, you will seem rushed as you try to type whatever the concern is.
- *Water bottles and coffee mugs:* If you and everyone else (excluding the parents) has water bottles or coffee mugs at a parental meeting, it is a tacit hint that you have something they don't; that you are part of a team and they are not.
- *Chewing gum*: Gnawing on a big wad of gum while speaking to a parent can be distracting and rude.
- *Not minding your personal space:* Should you be a person who tends to use touch and invading of personal space as a means of being warm and friendly to others, remember not everyone feels this is appropriate behavior. In fact, as there is a difference in power between the parents and you, they may feel intimidated or put off. This also has a cultural element to the morays of each persons culture as to the interaction that they have towards educators. Likewise, other unacceptable body language is also considered out of bounds.
- *Being late:* Even if you don't mind being late to your meetings, your student's parents will mind your wasting their time.
- *Talking in too much educational jargon:* Educational acronyms and abbreviations can lead to discomfort as a parent may not understand what you are saying and become frustrated.

WHISPERING, LAUGHING OR SNICKERING
IN FRONT OF A PARENT

- *Looking at your watch, phone, or texting:* This is an obvious point, but in the ever-connected world of the Internet, this is worth stating.
- An office that is pretentious, with degrees, numerous awards, and other items may intimidate a parent.
- Not enough eye contact or, in some cases culturally, too much eye contact.

PARENT PROGRAMS

Consider having a series of parenting programs or a "Parent University." It will allow parents to have an opportunity to meet with teachers. Programs that help with enriching parenting skills, especially with regard to disciplinary issues can help reduce stress in parents as they begin to view the school as an important partner in raising their child.

Also, it will allow a parent who has had bad experiences with principals as a student or has had "principal phobia" to see you as both an administrator and a person.

AVOID INSULATION

We have all had them; bosses who believed they were doing a great job. They sat in their offices very proud of what they were doing and believing that the school or company they ran was a virtual utopia. They slept well knowing that the school ran efficiently and that they were fair, responsible, and easy to approach. They do not need to ask or test this theory because they inherently know they are right.

The problem? They are dead wrong. They have convinced themselves without any information. Teachers, being well-meaning, insulate the administrators from these observations—either because they don't want to hurt their feelings or because they don't want to bother them. It becomes a dangerous path, however, because, when loyalty and school climate are tested, the administrators suddenly feel the tide turn on them and they are left hurt, dazed, and confused.

How does this affect parental exchanges? If you do not regularly test the waters of your school's climate, it may spill over to the parents, thus it becomes a difficult conversation at your door that you were previously blind to.

TO AVOID THIS INSULATION BE CERTAIN
TO DO THE FOLLOWING

- *Open up exchanges with faculty and parents who are open and honest without responding:* Just listen, absorb, and honestly critique yourself on what they are saying.
- *Allow anonymous comments (via a comment box or other such device) where you can read comments that are unvarnished and others can place them without fear of reprisal:* True, some of these comments may be petty with no merit, but others may just well be useful for you.
- *Invite those parent and staff with dissenting views or personalities to your own into meetings, committees, etc.* Why? Because then you will be able to get the alternate viewpoint to your own. That viewpoint may, at times, be correct and offer you a great counterbalance to those who simply act as "yes men" to anything you say.
- *Get out of your office:* Getting out of the four walls of your office allows you to see what is going on with your own two eyes. Do this at different times and on varying days so you can get an idea of what the environment truly looks like for everyone in the school. What you see may be vastly different from what you are told or believe.
- *Talk with everyone in your faculty to get the most balanced view of what is going on:* Speaking with paraprofessionals, secretaries, cafeteria workers, and custodians will give you the most balanced barometer of the educational climate of your facility.

NOTES

* "Olivier Theyskens Quote." BrainyQuote. Accessed April 10, 2016. http://www. brainyquote.com/quotes/quotes/o/olivierthe539947.html.

1. "N.J. Now Has More Than 100 School Religious Holidays You May Not Know About." Toms River, NJ Patch. 2016. Accessed April 12, 2016. http://patch. com/new-jersey/tomsriver/nj-approves-more-100-school-religious-holidays-you-may-not-know.

2. Gabor, Don. *How to Start a Conversation and Make Friends.* New York: Simon & Schuster, 2011.

3. Mehrabian, Albert. *Silent Messages: Implicit Communication of Emotions and Attitudes.* Belmont, CA: Wadsworth Pub., 1981.

4. "Triangulation (family Dynamics)." Psychology Wiki. Accessed February, 2016. http://psychology.wikia.com/wiki/Triangulation_(family_dynamics).

Chapter 6

Top Ten List

The Top Ten Most Challenging Parent/Family Types

Sometimes the only answer people are looking for when they ask for help is that they won't have to face the problem, alone.

—Mark Amend*

Every school and every district has them—challenging parents. These are the few, the 2% of parents who occupy 95% of your time. They leave you pulling out the few gray hair that you have left after a few years of having their children under your tutelage. I want to be clear, these are not your ordinary (the majority of) run-of-the-mill delightful parents. No, these are the difficult ones that earn reputations and make faculty and administrators alike cringe. They are scattered in every school district and, though their names and faces may be different, their behaviors, goals, and attitudes are markedly the same.

Before I discuss these parents I want something to be abundantly clear. The personality types of the parents below are stereotypes meant to highlight varying parental idiosyncractic traits of those you may find in a school setting.It is no way meant to be disrespectful to the parent(s). Parents have developed various ways of handling issues in order to get to the end result—providing their child what they need.

If you are a parent, you understand the highs and lows, the frustrations, as well as the rewards of your role. You also will know the heartbreak of when your child fails, when he or she is failed, or when he or she comes home feeling disappointed or sad. This is when we all do our very best to get what is needed for the child by any way possible. Each parent uses the tools they feel comfortable with to get what their child needs.

Likewise, the more tools you have at your disposal the better you are able to handle parental issues. If you only have one or two tools on your tool belt, you are limited in what you can fix. However, if you have a multitude of tools (including those out of your comfort zone), they will help determine your marketability in repairing challenging interactions.

THE TOP 13 DIFFICULT PARENTAL TYPES

1. *The "My child is an angel and you are all at fault" parent:* This is the parent who believes that their child is never, ever, at fault. It is the school, faculty, or students that somehow provoke and victimize their child (though it is proven time and time again that this is contrary to fact).

   • This parent tends to staunchly defend and protect their child from the potential of any natural or logical consequences. They equate protecting their son/daughter with defending him or her from any potential negative criticism (even when it is warranted). They will observe things in regard to their child in very "black and white" terminology. They will view teachers and administrators in a very concrete manner of great educator or bitter enemy, and hold their child to an impossibly high standard that most children could never reach.

   • Stick to the facts with these parents and avoid the pitfall of getting sucked into their emotional whirlpool. These families are often emotional when they come to see you and feel that they must stand up for their young child who is being "victimized." Mirroring anger, frustration, or emotion will only serve to add fuel to the proverbial fire with these mothers and fathers.

   • It is best when you deal with these parents to stick to a very strict and deliberate script to avoid getting wrapped up in the emotion when you have, in their belief, wronged their angelic child. If you can create a mantra with these parents in which you calmly repeat the statements you want to get across, this will somewhat quell their anger and strong emotion.

   • Document conversations each time. When they feel "victimized" (or worse, when their child has been a victim) they can become litigious to get justice for being wronged. Documentation of what has occurred and can occur (with both parent and student) can often help clarify facts as opposed to emotional exaggeration that often gets wrapped up in conflict or disagreement in these interventions.

   • These are conversations for which you want to have a clear framework of documentation detailing dates, times, and specific interactions. Again, avoid e-mail dialogues that can be used against you or misconstrued by these angered families who will tend to view any online communication in a negative light.

Rather, save e-mails for specific "one-way" communications in which you want to document something to these parents that you desire to make abundantly clear (for instance, disciplinary conversation, parental meeting, or failure of a parent to be present at a scheduled meeting).

- Children who are provided this type of "you are an angel" parenting will often "triangulate" parents against teachers, administrators, or other adults of authority (please see definition of "triangulation" discussed earlier). Be certain to have the student present in the conversation with these families in order to show him or her that parents cannot be pitted against the school without consequence.

In fact, these children have learned to play people against each other. They have learned that if they play the teacher against their parent they can slink away while the attention of all is shifted to the conflict. The payoff? The child learns that the consequence that was going to be applied is now forgotten in the fog of emotional discord that surrounds the situation.

- Avoid giving the student an opportunity to lie. Let's take a look at how we inadvertently encourage a child in this parenting style to be set up to lie by using a simplistic example: the child spills milk all over the tables in the lunchroom.

Immediately, we ask the child this question out of knee-jerk habit, "Did you spill that milk?" Now, the child has a choice: first the child could say he or she did it and risk a consequence or, second, lie and say he or she did not do it (after all you asked), and perhaps get out of any potential consequence on the off chance you believe him.

This latter strategy works well for these children in most parenting scenarios because often they are not directly told they are not being truthful. Therefore, if you know a child is not being truthful don't ask if he or she is being truthful; instead, address the issue that occurred directly.

Best conflict styles for this type of parent

- *"I Want to Be Friends with Everyone" Style:* By trying this style you extend an olive branch to indicate that you want to befriend these parents. Empathizing may help the parent to believe you understand the special nature of the child-parent relationship and their child's special qualities.
- *"Let's Figure This out Together" Style:* Cooperation may be a way to get the parent to separate the child's behavior from emotion, and be more willing to accept potential compromise.

Moderate conflict style for this type of parent

- ○ *"Conflict Avoider" Style:* It is acceptable to not engage in conflict with these parents initially. However, if continued parent-child conflicts ensue, you may eventually run into a larger issue leading to a blowout conflict down the road. This is due to the parent falsely taking your avoidance for acceptance.
- ○ *"You're Going to Listen and Follow What I Say or Else" Style:* If you dig your heels in with these parents, you will likely get immediate resistance. These parents want you to understand the special nature of the relationship they have with their child as well as the idiosyncratic importance of their child that versus other students. It is of no use to discuss the effect of the child on the other students in the class as the parent only has realistic interest in their own child.

2. *The "When in school he/she is your problem" parent:* Here is a parent that administrators, teachers, and other faculty will call and ask for assistance over and over again. The parents will either say that they will comply and don't, or will never contact you back. This is the parent that when you reach out to the contact numbers find the numbers are either wrong, disconnected, or you get no response.

- If a parent does not comply with helping you, do not immediately become defensive. Some of these parents are drowning in a world of financial despair or emotional, physical, or family issues. We cannot reasonably expect a parent to help you with making sure a child does his or her homework if the parents cannot keep electricity in their home (See Figure of Maslow's Hierarchy). First, see if the family's rudimentary survival needs are being met.
- If these basics (food, money, clothing, utilities) are not being met, offer to have the social worker or school counselor help them to get these needs addressed. If these needs are addressed, then the parents will have better ability to help you with what you need from them to work collaboratively for their child.
- These parents may believe that it is simply not their role to help with the child with regard to your concerns when he or she is at school. These parents look at their role as "I take care of my child when he or she is with me and don't ask you for help, so when my child is there with you he or she is solely your responsibility."
- Keep as current and as an expansive a list of emergency telephone numbers as possible as some of these parents change their phone numbers in quick succession. If this is the case, and you have tried numerous times to reach out to the family to no avail, cease trying. You are wasting your time, irritating your educators, and avoiding the development of

strategies within the school that can create rewards and consequences that are school-based versus inclusive of the home environment.

- How do you do this? Look for a large scope of rewards that can be provided to the child at school. Such rewards could be determined by asking students the following:
  - *Tell us 3 books/videos you want to read/watch at school*
  - *Tell us 3 activities you want to do at recess*
  - *Give us 3 tasks you want to do with your teacher*
  - *Tell us 3 things you would want to do if you had free time at school*
  - *Tell us 3 apps/books you would like to use at school*

Now, you have a pool of rewards that you can use and, consequently, take away if need be, that are internal to the school. This thereby provides effective interventions in the school to help the student succeed. Of course, documentation of issues should still be sent to the parent via certified mail (or e-mail) so that you have proof that they are in receipt of any necessary correspondence.

Best conflict styles for this type of parent:

- *"You're Going to Listen and Follow What I Say Or Else" Style:* This style is when you have to play hardball with a parent who absolutely refuses to enter the doorway of the school or participate in their child's learning. When it becomes an issue of safety to the student or others you must set strong boundaries and consequences to force these parents' hands in coming in.

Moderate conflict style for this type of parent:

- *"Conflict Avoider" Style:* Using this interpretation will create a neutral atmosphere within the parent-school interactions. These types of parents prefer not to have conflict or any significant level of conversation. Therefore, avoiding conflict (or most other interaction with the school) is specifically what they seek anyway.

Worst conflict styles for this type of parent:

- *"I Want to Be Friends with Everyone" Style:* These parents have no interest in being your friend or enemy. In fact, they just want you to, quite frankly, leave them alone when the child is in school. They have other items on their agenda that top anything you are going to tell them.
- *"Let's Figure This out Together" Style:* By nature of this parenting style, this very paradigm plays into what this parent does not want to do. These parents do not see a need or have a desire to work together

within the educational environment. Again, they are not adversarial; they just prefer to be an absent parent when it comes to contribution.

3. *The "know it all" parent:* These families are the questioners. They question why a teacher is doing something a certain way, why you as an administrator run your school in the manner you do, and why the district has chosen (or not chosen) a certain curriculum or testing system. They often are engineers or scientists and tend to be analytical. They navigate their world by inquiring about everything as a means of trying to understand something. However, this incessant inquiry could seem like uncertainty in your ability or that they are testing your knowledge.

- These parents want, and, indeed, need to know the curriculum and strategies you are using in class. These parents feel that comprehending as much about their child's learning makes them advocates and knowledgeable parents.

- Many times, parents of special education students, who feel that it is imperative to be knowledgeable advocates for their children, can seem to fall into this category. As the saying goes, "An informed customer is a good customer." These parents want to be as educated as the educators themselves. Their questioning, imparting their knowledge, or giving suggestions should not be confused for criticism. Be careful not take this advice personally or as a questioning of your competence.

- *Such parents would benefit from programs on curriculum and more frequent parent-teacher contact:* These parents are constantly seeking information on what their child is learning, what is out there, and what to expect and anticipate for the future. Providing these answers on the district website, in newsletters, or in conferences, help alleviate some of the concerns of a lack of understanding of what their child is learning.

- *Encourage teachers to notify parents in writing when they are deviating from the curriculum:* This must be done especially if there are any items that could be deemed in the least bit controversial (and, of course, parents should also be notified that they reviewed these with the administration ahead of time).

Best conflict styles for this type of parent:

- ○ *"I Want to Be Friends with Everyone" Style:* If you determine to understand what the parent is trying to tell you and work as pseudo colleagues to comprehend what they are trying to profess to you, they will be honored to teach and befriend you. This may also allow an entrance for you to get your viewpoint across.

Moderate conflict style for this type of parent:

- ○ *"Let's Figure This out Together" Style:* If you allow parents to believe they know more than you, they will continue to educate you on how to figure things out from their perspective. Some of these parents have a difficulty with compromise because they don't see the value of your participation or view your suggestions as valid as their own. You must carefully then turn the tide from their telling you how to figure issues out to collaborating on observations and potential suggestions for interventions.
- ○ *"You're Going to Listen and Follow What I Say or Else" Style:* Keep in mind, these persons are not normally conflictual. Rather, they have difficulty accepting that others (even "professionals") may be able to add to what they see as the solely correct view. Harsh approaches may take them off guard and cause them to shut down as they may become greatly offended very quickly.

4. *The "bully" parent:* In the news there has been a great deal of talk about harassment, intimidation, and bullying in the school environment. What is often neglected, however, is that sometimes the apple does not fall far from the proverbial tree. Bullying and pushy behavior can be a learned behavior. Here is how to deal with these parents:
   - *Be proactive.* Do not wait for this child to go home and state what he or she feels happened in a particular situation. This gives ample time for the parents' anger to grow. You might say, "Well don't they want to hear the other side of the story?" No, emotion is not logic and anger is the emotion du jour. Call the parents and allow your side of the story to sink in before the student gets home.
   - *Do not call these parents when you are angered.* This can lead to a confrontation with these families. They are often angered and when they are confronted with anger (even the slightest tone) they key in on this which can lead to an explosive confrontation.
   - *DO NOT e-mail these parents.* Remember when you have read or received an e-mail or text and misread the context behind what the sender was saying (or vice versa)? When you e-mail these parents they often believe a confrontational tone is taken even when none was intended. Also, e-mails can be manipulated to have different meanings and are hard copy documentation. Calling and documenting provides a one-way form of certification that is to your advantage.
   - *If you believe a meeting is going to become explosive, make sure that you alert a resource/security officer.* If it does become explosive or overly emotional, stop the meeting and consider rescheduling it. If steam is coming out of the ears there is nothing productive going into the brain.

- *Avoid allowing these families to back you into a corner in which you feel you may have to compromise your values or integrity.* Often, these parents will try to force their point of view over issues. First, they may attempt to get small issues pushed across, then, when they pick up steam and find this strategy works for them, they will attempt to push their agenda in larger, more important, issues.
- If you suspect that you are dealing with a "bully" type of parent, establish strong boundaries at the start and they are much more likely to respect these. If you don't you will find yourself playing catch-up and trying to maintain boundaries with these parents who will point out, "But you (or someone else in charge) made an exception last time." These parents will only respect strength from the outset; other strategies are perceived as weakness.

Best conflict styles for this type of parent:

- ○ *"Let's Figure This out Together" Style:* As long as you determine ahead what areas of your educational values and vision you are not willing to be pushed or compromise on, this is an adequate strategy. Be firm on what areas you are willing to negotiate and let them know fostering a deal does not involving giving in on your values, policies, or vision for your students or school.

Moderate conflict style for this type of parent:

- ○ *"You're Going to Listen and Follow What I Say or Else" Style:* This interactional type can go in either direction with this parental style. Why? Because if you use this, initially the "bully" parent sees this as a battle and an ineffective power struggle ensues. That being said, however, if you are the educator who has seen these parents steamroll over others and get their way by fear mongering you may have no choice but to divert to this method. The trouble occurs when previous educators have given up school vision and values for the sake of keeping the peace. Now, you must set very strict boundaries because you are backed into a corner and must step forward to represent what is best educationally. These parents are certain to argue and bring up the lack of the school system's/faculty's consistency in this case.

Worst conflict style for this type of parent:

- ○ *"I Want To Be Friends With Everyone" Style:* The "bully" type parent mistakes kindness and flexibility for weakness. This may be acceptable when it comes to small issues, however, the saying of "giving an inch taking a mile" is clear here. The difficulty is that after many miles of stepping back you find your back against the wall until you cannot give anymore. The parents believes at this point that your giving is an entitlement and will fight even harder to try to climb over a wall that they perceive as having previously been weak.

5. *The "My child will attend school when they want to" parent:*
   - *Look for patterns of absences in children to see if they are after/before weekends or holidays? Are they sporadic? Is there a pattern?* If they are absent after weekends this may be a parental issue of parents simply being unable or unwilling to get up after a long weekend.
   - *Sometimes teachers will refuse to provide work to students who are chronically absent.* This is counterproductive as it does not allow a student who may want to keep up with work the ability to do so. Insist that schoolwork be provided as long as the parent picks it up from the school. Remind teachers' their vision is to teach all of our students, not withhold education.
   - *Look to be sure that no patterns of abuse or neglect are occurring.* Sometimes, unfortunately, students are kept home to allow bruises to heal or because parents are not present physically or emotionally to put a student on the bus. Does the child wear long sleeves in warm weather? Are any bruises noted or physical punishment discussed? Does the student (who is younger) indicate that he or she cannot wake up their parent or that he or she put himself or herself on the bus? Does the student bring no, inappropriate, or spoiled foods/snacks to eat? These are all red flags.
   - *Sometimes students do have true school phobia.* If so, when they do come to school let them feel welcomed. Do not shame the student or have yourself or their peers ask questions as to where he or she was. Doing so with others around only serves to exacerbate anxiety issues. Seek assistance from your school social worker or counselor. Even consider speaking to the school social worker/counselor about discussing outpatient counseling. Should the child be receiving outside counseling, secure a release of information so that you could use some of their strategies within the school setting as well.
   - *Is the parent home?* As noted earlier, if the parent is home this is one of the tell-tale signs that a student will want to stay in the house. Students often will feel they are missing something that a parent is doing when he or she is home. If a parent has a chronic illness the child may find the need to help him or her. Assuring the child (as well as the parent) of the legal and educational role of a student being in school is vital. Additionally, letting both parties know the responsive family member will be okay is crucial.

- *Involve the attendance officer early.* The attendance officer can often give you a glimpse into what may be occurring within the residence that you may not have an awareness of otherwise. Regular discussions with the attendance officer after this will determine whether you need to take further steps such as contacting family services or reaching out and providing additional, vital supports.
- *Look to see if absences are due to an understandable pattern.* Oftentimes after long times off of school (i.e., holidays) or after the summer you will typically see students having school refusal. It is less typical when children have absences in the middle of a week or toward the middle to end of an academic year.

Best conflict styles for this type of parent:

- *"I Want to Be Friends with Everyone" Style:* Many of these parents have significant anxiety themselves. They worry what can happen when their child is out of their sight and so they keep their child home like a security blanket. They also give subtle cues to their child that they need to be home with them and may even reward the child for doing so (despite denying this to the contrary with educational staff). A listening ear for this anxiety and fear may go a long way to break the ice in their revealing this truth, which they find an embarrassing, yet realistic, situation.

Moderate conflict style for this type of parent:

- *"Let's Figure This out Together" Style:* These parents, above all, want to be listened to. They want you to know the worst case scenarios that they believe could occur are real to them. They want you to understand that their child needs them and vice versa and they want you to comprehend that, to them, their anxiety is as real as that yellow school bus that arrives to kidnap their child each day.
- *"You're Going to Listen and Follow What I Say or Else" Style:* Ordinarily, this style may create more of an anxious stir and ultimate shutdown when in direct confrontation with these worrisome parents. There is a vital and substantial exclusion, however, when a small percentage of these parents are physically abusive.

  They use keeping the child home as a way of harboring him or her to allow bruises to heal from abuse. In this rare case, you must set strong criteria that the appropriate authorities must (and will) be called immediately.

Worst conflict style for this type of parent:

- *Avoiding Conflict at All Costs:* If you avoid the conflict of dealing with these parents, they will be happy. Their anxiety is only heightened by confrontation and conflict. Unfortunately, sometimes the attendance officer going to the home or your contacting them may be the push they need to get over the seemingly unsurmountable mountain of anticipatory anxiety that they experience daily.

6. *The "Not my child" parent:* This mother or father indicates that their child would never do what you are indicating that they did. They seem to have difficulty accepting that their child is responsible for anything because they see their child in the limited lens of within their home without any other peer interactions or any responsibilities (i.e., schoolwork) placed upon him or her.

- *Educate the family on board policies and procedures.* This takes the conversation away from blaming and toward rules and regulations. These parents often believe you are "victimizing" their child and so they will try to turn anything that deviates from these black-and-white discussions into a personal attack against them, their child, and their family.
- *Allow the parents to address their concerns first.* This allows you to "take some wind out of their sails," so to speak, and then remind them, in a firm, yet understanding tone that the rules of the school apply even if they/we don't necessarily accept all of them. If you agree with any point of their argument be careful to not let them take this to mean that you agree that they are correct that their child is right (just that you understand their viewpoint). "Not my child" parents are looking for you to agree and be an ally to them and so they are hanging on every word that indicates you are with them in the conflict at hand.
- *You may want to have another faculty member (such as the assistant principal or school social worker) to have further documentation of these meetings should the parents take it to another level.* These parents can become angry quickly so plan accordingly.

Best conflict styles for this type of parent:

- ○ *"Let's Figure This out Together" Style:* Cooperation is by far the best way to deal with these kinds of families. They believe that their child can do no wrong and you have evidence to the contrary. If you try to understand that they see their child as for the most part good, and are looking to solve a problem without criticizing the child as a whole, it will go a long way toward working with these particular parents.

Moderate conflict style for this type of parent:

- ○ *"I Want to Be Friends with Everyone" Style:* This may work initially with these parents as you attempt to first join with them positively. Just remember that these parents will swing wildly when it comes to the defense of their child. Therefore, do not confuse friendliness with priority and loyalties.

Worst conflict style for this type of parent:

○ *"Conflict Avoider" Style:* Since this parent does not believe that their child is at fault or blame if you avoid conflict then you will simply confirm the parent's belief that "it is not my child." However, the parent will generally discipline the child with the "wait until we get home" attitude so you will not need to lose valuable relational ammunition wasting it on a parent with seemingly conflictual attitudes to your suggestions.

7. *The "passive-aggressive" parent:* These parents can be especially dangerous. They can be heavily involved in the school, in organizations, and social media. They may troll the school for gossip or to establish dual relationships with teachers as educators and friends.

   • *Be aware of gifts, even small ones.* If a teacher or administrator is accepting gifts (even small ones) such as the daily coffee or bagel, there may be a price to pay. This is not to say these parents don't always do this out of the goodness of their hearts; some are using this to establish an account of obligation for the educator or administrator. The seemingly inexpensive token of appreciation then becomes more of an expensive gift of trying to establish a bond. It is much like the apple put on a teacher's desk hoping to be the teacher's pet.

   • *Be careful of backhanded compliments.* A passive-aggressive parent will compliment you by comparing you to another faculty member/administrator. "You are a much better principal than Ms. so and so." By not defending the other, or by accepting this compliment inadvertently, you may set up this parent to state that you agree with his or her view of the other.

   • *Remember again, the pendulum swings both ways with these parents.* These parents are black and white with very few shades of gray. If you are "the best principal ever" and they sing your praises or those of your faculty members, be cautious and slightly afraid. They are also likely to swing the other way and indicate that you/they are "the worst ever." As proof of this, look at the history that these parents have left behind with administrators and teachers. If you see a trail of teachers that have been bad-mouthed, and who the parents state were unjust to their family or their child, it may be coincidental, but, it may also be that it is just a matter of time before you are tossed aside into the bin of "bad" educators who did not see their point of view and who betrayed them despite their kindness previously extended to you.

- *Avoid, at all costs, social media or the soccer field.* These parents are often involved in many community organizations and in social media. By getting entangled in any situation with these parents and not maintaining strong boundaries (and advising faculty to do the same), you may be in for a whole world of hurt. The judgmental and gossip-filled world of social media and the field of soccer moms and dads is their home field. These parents also like to volunteer and can often be found in places where teachers congregate (i.e., the faculty room, work room, etc.) They are not usually invited into these areas, however, they know this is where they can get the latest school gossip. Be warned and warn your faculty accordingly.

Best conflict styles for this type of parent:

- *"Let's Figure This Out Together" Style:* Using this method is likely the best with a few important caveats: be sure you have strong boundaries, do not fall for false praise, and do not allow these parents to bad-mouth anybody. Let them know that only direct communication with every respective party involved will be tolerated.

Moderate conflict style for this type of parent:

- *"Conflict Avoider" Style:* It is the nature of people with this type of personality to not directly focus anger and aggression (hence "passive-aggressive"). When you approach these parents with anger or conflict directly they will back down. This is a temporary solution, though; the next thing you will find is that they will seek other ways of vengeance via social media, bad-mouthing you to the PTA, or another indirect means of venting their wrath.

Worst conflict style for this type of parent:

- *"I Want to Be Friends with Everyone" Style:* These parents' main strategy is to cozy up to others to get what they want. The use of your first name, purchasing coffee or lunch for you, and volunteering in your classroom are all attempts to blur the line between professional and peer. Therefore, if you attempt at all to be overly friendly, they take this as an opportunity to be friends. Being friends means that the boundaries of appropriate and inappropriate as well as the role of teacher versus parents now becomes murky and you can enter danger ethical territory.

8. *The "why does everyone always pick on my child" parent:* These parents are the opposite of the bullying parents at first glance. They question why their child is always victimized either by the students, the faculty, or

both. Oftentimes, however, these parents can become "bullying" parents or "not my child" parents depending on how the issue and relationship evolves or dissolves:

- *Do not allow parents to take the conversation of behavioral issues with their child toward blaming or victimization.* Remind them that it is the behavior that you are addressing and that you are not condemning their child's character or, consequently, the alleged bully parents' parenting skills. If you do so, it goes down a bumpy emotional road and provides little in the way of solutions.
- *Avoid using too much emotionality or overstating things.* Too much talking or reactivity muddies the water with these families and only makes them feel more victimized and attacked. Listening carefully and not adding too much in the way of emotions or words is critically important with these parents.
- *Encourage rules and consequences that are consistent across classrooms.* It is difficult to enforce rules and consequences when each teacher has vastly differing standards. Be certain that your teachers have somewhat consistent rules and consequences among each class. Why? Because how can you enforce rules and consequences in a school when each classroom has their own manner of each? Further, this allows these parents to state that the school is inconsistent in its handling of issues (and they would be correct in this assessment).

Best conflict styles for this type of parent:

- ○ *"I Want to Be Friends with Everyone" Style:* These parents are afraid that their child is being victimized. With the secretive nature of harassment, intimidation, and bullying it can very well be that their child is, in fact, being bullied. This is especially true with girl-on-girl bullying that is harder to root out and more devious. The first thing these parents need is a friendly ear to listen to their concerns.

Moderate conflict style for this type of parent:

- ○ *"Let's Figure This out Together" Style:* On the surface, working together may be useful. However, remember that these parents see their child as victimized and some are out for blood. They may bring up another student's name or issues within the neighborhood of vendettas that spill over into school. Be respectful of the privacy of the other party. Avoid mentioning names, identifying information/characteristics, or disciplinary consequences that occurred with the other student (or students). Be careful, because these parents are masters at baiting you to discuss other students/parents and throwing the issue of their child and their involvement off track.

Worst conflict style for this parental type:

○ *"Conflict Avoider" Style:* These parents already see a conflict in that their child is being victimized. Whether or not there is an actual conflict and to what degree is no matter, they still see that their child is being hurt. If you avoid addressing this issue these parents will not hesitate to go above your head to reach a conclusion to protect their child from the onslaught of bullying that they fear is going on. Therefore, you should address the conflict directly with the victim's family and it must be investigated and dealt with in an expedited fashion.

Additionally, in many states, harassment, intimidation, and bullying laws indicate you must deal with these issues within a designated time frame. They also have strict consequences that can be applied for a lack of investigation or delay in these types of issues.

9. *The "helicopter" parent:* These parents are so named for their tendency to "hover" around their child. They may be considered over involved or over indulgent and often do not let their child grow or develop to age-appropriate expectations. This is generally because they are anxiety-ridden about their child's growth and well-being. These children may be emotionally immature or sneaky in order to avoid having to deal with the rigid and inflexible rules and overly watchful eyes of their parents.
   • *These parents do not trust that their child is safe or capable nor that faculty initially can be trusted with their child's safety.* Contact the parents (or have the teacher or school counselor do so) on a regular basis initially to assure them that their child is doing well, then taper back. Some administrators might argue that they do not have time to do this. Trust me, if you do not call these families at your convenience you will get calls from the parents of an "urgent" nature frequently at their convenience.
   • *Compliment the families for their earnest concern for their child.* Remember they are hovering over their children due not only to worry but also out of a deep and passionate concern for their well-being.
   • *Note successes and report these to the parents.* These families are concerned that their children will not be able to handle the proverbial "real world" without their intervention. Successes then have to be reported to parents to allow them to realize that they do not have to do everything for their children because they are capable of doing tasks independently.
   • *Call these parents immediately when they call you.* These parents hover because they are anxious and believe at any time a seemingly small issue can be a calamity for their child. If you call them and leave a

message assure them that the call is NOT an emergency. If they call you, try to call them back as soon as possible. If you do not, they are likely to go up the chain of command trying to get an answer to, what they believe, is an urgent issue that must be handled immediately.

Best conflict styles for this type of parent:

- ○ *"Let's Figure This out Together" Style:* These parents want constant reassurance to know their child is okay. How you do this, how often, and by what means will determine how comfortable the parents feel. If they feel comfortable this, in turn, allows them to somewhat loosen the reins of worry from their child as the year carries forward.

Moderate conflict style for this type of parent:

- ○ *"I Want to Be Friends with Everyone" Style:* These parents believe that their child will have difficulty handling any issue that comes down the pike. They are one step graduated from the "my child will attend school when they want to" parents in that they believe that their child needs them and vice versa. However, they provide you more trust by actually "letting" their child attend school. Therefore, by showing friendliness to these parents you are assuring them that their child will be okay.
- ○ *"Conflict Avoider" Style:* These parents are very reluctant to entrust their child to the hands of anyone they believe will not give him or her a soft place to fall. A conflict will only add to their dismay that their child will not be able to handle the mean, cruel real world that lies ahead of them in the educational setting.

Worst conflict style for this type of parent:

- ○ *"You're Going to Listen and Follow What I Say or Else" Style:* If you use this style the parents will retreat and the "helicopter" nature of their behavior will only increase. These parents are apprehensive about letting their child out the door and into the doorways of your school. If you throw up rigid verbal boundaries they will flee. They are desperate to know that they can somehow still monitor their child in some way to be certain they are okay. This is especially evident in younger, primary-level parents who have not had an opportunity to have their child spread their wings.

10. *The "distrustful of public education/special education" Parent:* Some of our parents have had bad experiences with public education themselves. Whether it is because of academic issues, a lack of focus on public education, or having been in the special education system themselves, some parents are not inherently trusting of public schools, administrators, or

teachers. For this very reason, they come in ready to fight, with an attitude that is one of defensiveness:

- *Avoid having meetings in which several people are saying the same thing to the parent that is negative or critical of their child.* How many meetings have you attended in which five faculty members say the same thing about how a student is performing poorly in school? If one person says this, it does not have to be echoed by everyone else. Therefore, prepare ahead as to who will say what.
- *Don't focus on being right or wrong, focus on what is right for the student.* Oftentimes the parents or faculty members get trapped in "being right." We must ask ourselves, if we engage in that power struggle what are we doing productively that is "right" for the student?
- *Look for opportunities of mutual gain.* If we can have the parents "save face" and if we find a chance for us to meet half-way with these families, that is the optimal solution or what is often called a "win-win" solution.
- *Some of these parents may have been in special education programs themselves.* If you are going to suggest that their child is going to be classified or referred for special education, this will bring back memories of the archaic experiences they had as a child. Therefore, if you are going to discuss that special education is not the same as when they were children, you must show them how it is different. They need to see what kind of class their child will be in as they are skeptical of a system that they felt segregated them from so-called "normal" children.

Best conflict styles for this type of parent:

- ○ *"I Want to Be Friends with Everyone" Style:* Befriending these parents is vital. They are grieving that their child may have limits to varying degrees. This means recognizing that the some of the hopes they had for their child may have to be modified. If your child was stricken with a physical disability it would be a similar process. Someone who can sit by these parents and listen is a necessary element in securing what is best for their child.
- ○ *"Let's Figure This out Together" Style:* As we stated earlier, many of these parents have a misconceived notion of what special education is like based on past, outdated models. Therefore, having family members be a part of the process and having them witness what special education classrooms are like with their own eyes will help to facilitate a bond of trust and cooperation.

Worst conflict style for this type of parent:

- ○ *"Conflict Avoider" Style:* We do not want to avoid conflict altogether with these parents. If a mother or father has a grossly distorted view of what their child is capable of doing, we may have to address this directly. If their view (well-meaningly) goes against what is best for the child, the other students, or the values and mission of your school, then you have no choice but to engage in tactful conflict resolution. If we do not do so we are wasting valuable time that is critical for the student's, and perhaps their peers', learning. Of course, we must proceed carefully through the web of special education laws and board policies and procedures.

11. *The "my kid is bored" parent:* This is a favorite excuse of parents who are told that their child is not living up to the academic rigors of a particular class. This myth has been fostered due to a number of different issues.
    - *First, if a parent asks a child, "what did you today in school?" what is the response?* As you know, if you have children (or have ever asked this question), the answer is usually some variant of "nothing," "I don't know," or "not much." It is no wonder then parents would say their child is bored. If nothing has broken the memory threshold of anything interesting, then what would you think?
    - *It is important that we have constant communication with parents via newsletters, phone calls, or websites that offer consistent and constant information of the school day.* Further, if we suggest that parents ask pointed questions (for e.g., "I saw you read about whales today, can you tell me about that?") they will have a better gauge of what their child is doing in school and will be less inclined to take verbatim that if their child says "we did nothing in school" that is, in fact, the case.
    - *It is important to remind parents that the responsibilities of a student are to know the information and be able to recite what is needed.* If you provide them with an example in their own lives or occupations, it is useful. If you cannot be productive in your job role, the fact is, your abilities are not useful.
    - *Consider that perhaps these students may perform better with technology as a means of demonstrating their academic abilities. For instance, they tend to be "bored" because their brains are wired into the world of technology, which is more visual and tactile in nature than an average classroom lesson.* If possible, try to have the teacher use technology to see if the student will produce work more frequently. If so, the student could later be weaned back into traditional academics again.
    - *Assessing a child to understand what his or her strengths are and where his or her weaknesses lie may give you a good summative assessment of a realistic, unbiased approach, and inform all parties as to what is going on.* If it is, in fact, boredom (which is usually on the lower realms of possibilities) then consider using more tactile strategies versus auditory or visual learning paradigms. Children with low attention spans,

from my experience, tend to be better tactile learners and worse at visual and auditory comprehension. Unfortunately, we tend to use the latter to teach these students as their paradigm fits more within most teachers' comfort levels.

Best conflict styles for this type of parent:

○ *"Let's Figure This out Together" Style:* These parents are seeking legal recourse. If you can look like you are cooperating prior to going down this tenuous road, it would be a much better strategy to the potential alternative. Figuring things out, however, is not an end in itself. Be certain you have legal representation and documentation should things go south.

Moderate conflict style for this type of parent:

○ *"Conflict Avoider" Style:* Just because a family is seeking legal recourse does not mean you avoid conflict. It is certainly a goal to end things amicably without the hassle of legal and court issues. However, do not allow idle threats to back you into a corner and make you compromise on education, your values, or vision.

Worst conflict style for this type of parent:

○ *"Conflict Avoider" Style:* At times we try to avoid conflict with these parents. However, we must find out what are the reasons that create a conflict between having the aptitude to do the work and what triggers the avoidance or refusal to create the finished product.

12. *The "legal eagle" parent type:* These parents are seeking legal ramifications because they feel their attempts at working within the school parameters have been thwarted and they often see no other viable option(s). These parents initially may, or may not, have been litigious, but now they have reached that step.

Best conflict styles for this type of parent:

○ *"Let's Figure This out Together" Style:* If you take this approach you can utilize it to figure out the vast gap between knowledge and production of classwork. The parents believe their child is capable, however, since he or she cannot be productive, this creates a source of great frustration. Therefore, we must find a middle ground in which we determine that their child may, in fact, be unable to produce the work needed at school because of not being capable, may need more help not unlike the close supervision they receive at home or, much less likely, that they are in fact bored. Any of these possibilities will take parental trust and patience, which is why this is a good approach.

Moderate conflict style for this type of parent:

○ *"I Want to Be Friends with Everyone" Style:* Here is the difficulty; if you attempt to befriend the parents who are saying that you are not capable of lighting a fire under the child for motivation, this is challenging. This leads to some challenging conversations involving a teaching style or school climate that can seem personal. Despite an educator being told that his or her inability to motivate a child is "nothing personal," everything about it is personal. Separating a child's lack or inability to produce work from the parents' unrealistic attitude about the child's aptitude can be tough.

Worst conflict style for this type of parent:

○ *"I Want to Be Friends with Everyone" Style:* With "legal eagle" style parents, do not be lulled into a feeling that you are friends. You both have a goal, which is to determine what is best for the educational decision; however, the parents are seeking what is best for their child and you are looking at the bigger picture. Loyalties are divided between both parties and being cordial should not be confused with the crossing or blurring of boundaries.

13. *The impaired parent:* If you run into a parent who is impaired due to alcohol, drugs, or mental illness, this represents an obvious, very serious issue for the child. The sad fact is that some parents are so saddled with their own issues that their ability to take care of themselves is significantly compromised and they are therefore unable to help their child as well.

Best conflict styles for this type of parent:

○ *Unfortunately, there is only a single way to handle these issues.* If you suspect abuse or neglect of a child, you must contact your local division of family youth services. It is not appropriate to investigate this case as this will further complicate the agency's investigation. If you are not certain about the specifics of how to do so, contact your social worker or guidance counselor who can take you through the process of alerting the division of family services accordingly. They can also point out to signs and symptoms of possible mental illness, and alcohol or drug abuse.

Many of us ask: When should we contact child protective services? The answer is when you begin to suspect child abuse or neglect. Remember, you are not there to answer the question; you are there to say I have a reasonable belief to know that this could be abuse or neglect and then refer the case immediately as this is (in almost every state) a legal mandate with legal and possible licensing consequences.

Keep in mind, that it is better to contact protective services as early as possible. Though laws vary from state to state, many of the child protection workers prefer to interview a child in school. This environment is safe for all involved and it prevents the child from being coached by the parents when they get home.

Needless to say, these children need extra tender loving care (TLC). Additionally, if you suspect abuse, you should be cautious of what you tell the parents. If you know that a parent has a history of abusive behavior, you may want to think carefully about how you contact these parents in regard to disciplinary issues.

KEEP IN MIND WITH ALL PARENTS

It's always the people who know the least about you who want to judge you the most.

—Anonymous

We are working with families, but we only have a glimpse of the situations they are in. We work with mothers and fathers who don't have basic utilities, who struggle to put food on the table, who are overwhelmed by the emotional or medical issues of their children, spouse, or themselves. Some parents are those who never had the support system you have or the opportunity to strive for the education you received.

True, some of these situations may have been, for some, their own doing. However, remember that the child had no control of the situation and you must go through the parent to educate the child. That being said, it is also important to remember your judging can be a barrier that or place an obstacle in communication with the parent. In short, you don't know, and will never know, what fully goes on in the household or be able to understand what the parent is going through. The same can be said of that family's understanding the challenges that occur for you personally and within your classroom as well.

Please know that these parental types only represent a handful of the parents you may work with. Try to remember that many of these parents may be drowning in a sea of frustration or emotional, physical, and/or financial issues. Therefore, they will pull down anyone, or anything, that is around them (including you) in an attempt to keep their heads above water.

When you interact with these parents, think about the priorities. You only have a limited amount of ammunition and power and so you must decide if this is the issue/hill that you want to die on regarding a parental concern. If you are working with these parents, give them productive ideas as opposed to telling them what their child can't do or what their child's limitations are. Remind them that the goal of the school and the parents are ultimately the same: to do what is right for their child.

NOTE

* @vflahert. "Asking for Help." Leading With Intention. N.P. Web. 16 May. 2016

Chapter 7

Prevailing with Parents

Understanding, Involving, and Interacting with Challenging Parents

In teaching, you can't do the Bloom stuff until you take care of the Maslow stuff.

—Alan E. Beck*

"We always have the same parents!" It's a frequent complaint year after year when conducting parenting enrichment and educational programs for the school district. Our "role model parents" were the only ones who attended. They seemed so adept at parenting that often you feel you learned more from them than they did from you. Soon you begin to ask—how can we increase attendance at our parenting programs, and, more important, how do we get our "at risk parents" to come? Working with other school counselors and school social workers, we have discovered that the following strategies helped to get some new faces to attend our events—and to keep them coming back again and again.

First, it is important to understand where many of the more demanding, "at risk" parents are in their life journey. Let's go back to our basic college psychology coursework and Maslow's Hierarchy of Needs (figure 7.1). Basically, it states that we must first meet our physiological needs—the basics of life such as food, shelter, and sleep. So we must ask ourselves, if a parent is unhealthy (either physically or emotionally), cannot put food on the table, or works many jobs just to keep the lights on in the house, can he or she meet the other varied needs of himself or herself or his or her children?

Next is the need for shelter; if you live in a home that is bug-infested, in disrepair, or does not have the basics of running water, heat, and electricity because the utilities are in a constant state of being turned on and off due to the inability to pay, how do you make a parent-teacher conference?

83

These are often the state of the homes of many of our most "at risk" parents. If you think you are in an affluent district and this does not occur, think again. It only takes a missed bill, a job loss, chronic illness, or substance abuse to put many families on the edge of this precipice. It is important that we are aware of these needs and how they affect our families to avoid judging too quickly. Parent resistance to helping the school may in reality simply be a matter of survival and making some very hard choices of priority.

Go to where they are.

Look at where the majority of your at-risk students live, and hold the programs at those locations. Sometimes you can find a condo, apartment complex, clubhouse, or community center to give you the space at no cost by helping them see the benefit of improved parenting skills in their community. Parents who use enriched parenting skills are parents who are less apt to have children who will use their idle time toward destructive or disruptive behavior in their neighborhoods. This is, in a term made popular in Stephen Covey's *Seven Habits of Highly Effective People*, a win-win for everyone and should be marketed as such.[1]

Offer food/dinner.

Food equals attendance (i.e., if you feed them they will come). Dinner is one less meal that a parent has to prepare. This is especially important when

Figure 7.1

families have to struggle to find money for food (see figure 7.1). Also, attendance tends to be better toward the end of a month when food stamps may be exhausted. Sometimes local restaurants may even consider donations in exchange for free advertising. This may be an area in which you may solicit your school's PTA/PTO or Booster Club to offer a complimentary ad in exchange for their sponsoring a meal or snack.

Have children and parents involved at the same time.

When children are involved, parents are usually not far behind. If you can encourage the children to be excited about an activity, then you may just have to schedule your parenting enrichment program at the same time. An activity or tutoring time gives parents the thrust they need to come to a program. Additionally, if you schedule your parenting enrichment program before an evening concert, play, or assembly the children are in, parents may be apt "killing two birds with one stone" and attend both.

Choose topics that are long on practicality and shorten theory.

Parents who are struggling to keep their heads above water are most interested in what they can use right now. Keep topics current and create a curriculum that addresses the most practical, short topics. Break the topics down so they can be handled in one night (e.g., "How to Deal with Temper Tantrums" or "How to Get Your Child to Listen"). Session titles that are too vague or too complex such as "Family Communication" will not generate as much interest.

Now you may be one to ask, how is this educational? We want to provide information on core curriculum standards or on preparing for the next standardized testing. While this is true, we must first find a topic that parents will "bite on." Standardized testing or curriculum standards may not be something of interest if your child is having a tantrum every time you turn around and you cannot go anywhere or get anything done. If you introduce something that is immediately applicable in their lives as parents and then introduce them to the educational concerns once they get involved, you are likely to get a better response overall.

Offer other resources as well.

Most at-risk parents are dealing with difficult issues such as unemployment, illness, abuse, etc. If possible, ask local social service agencies to be present so they can answer questions and distribute appropriate materials.

If you have a "one stop" shop in your parenting program such as a resource fair in which one or two organizations attend each workshop, you will be able to provide parents a means of getting much-needed resources. Some parents may not have the ability to get to the resources, and bringing those to them provides the necessary and vital supports for them to, hopefully, address core needs. This allows them to then focus on other concerns such as how to be an important member of the team involved in their child's education. This will also help address fulfilling the most basic needs that may be lacking.

Advertise everywhere.

Sending a flier home with a child usually won't cut it, so you need to work harder to get the word out. Find out where these parents look at fliers (community centers, libraries, grocery stores). The best thing to do is to make individual phone calls to the parents you want there. Does it take more time? Yes, but it is better than wasting your time conducting a program in a roomful of empty chairs. Also, be sure to encourage those who did attend to spread the word to other parents.

Make it fun.

Think of activities that parents and children can do together. Make it memorable for both parties. If one is an "at risk" parent, one may be struggling just to keep his or her family's heads above water. Stress and anxiety do not leave a lot of time for things like family dinners and memorable activities. This may be a need that can be partially fulfilled in parental enrichment programs, as a much-needed break from the tsunami-like waves of stress.

Involve the teachers.

Ask teachers to give out extra homework passes to students whose parents attend. Encourage students by having their teachers (who are usually the most familiar, stable figures in a child's academic life) to be present at the programs. This also gives the teachers an insight into the diverse environments and circumstances in which our students reside.

Give things away.

Check your district's policy on giveaways first, but sometimes the PTA will help with door prizes or other freebies the parents and children can take home. Occasionally, local businesses will make donations as well.

No RSVP.

You probably won't get an accurate number anyway. The last thing that an "at risk" parent is likely to do is call and RSVP (again, see figure 2.0). Why? With a frenetic schedule and all that is on their radar screens, it is unlikely that you will even get a return phone call, let alone an RSVP. This will also give families an opportunity to informally invite other parents as well. If you are concerned that you may not have a concrete number for the first workshop, aim high and then adjust from there.

Keep it short:

The actual parenting enrichment program should not be longer than an hour. Focus on quality versus quantity. Remember, however, to add time for a question-and-answer period.

Call and say "thank you."

Have a sign-in sheet so you can call to thank those parents who attended. This will also be your list to call when promoting the next program session. You may ask, "Why do I have to thank parents for coming to a program for them?" Because they, like you, took time out of their schedule. Additionally, they are the customers whose support trickles down to our ultimate goal, which is education of the students that we have a mutual investment in.

Look for grants.

You may be able to find private grants to fund some of your parenting programs. If your district has a designated grant writer, this person may be helpful. Otherwise, seek local agencies and organizations that fund community grants. Oftentimes, money obstacles can be a matter of a simple redirection of resources that would otherwise go unspent and unused.

Encourage don't discourage.

It goes without saying that parenting programs should be positive. Let parents know that you are trying to enrich the skills they have, not criticize, judge, or monitor what they already do. Many parents have had bad experiences with schools, child protective services, or other agencies or institutions. Don't turn them off by complaining about the job they are doing. Often they are trying the best with what they have. True, some are burned out and may seem disinterested; however, just like we would for the disengaged student, we must try to "light a spark." Lighting a spark in a parent may be the wick you need to light a spark in the student as well. Or put another way, as an esteemed colleague stated, "Even broken crayons can still color."

Make social service agencies aware of your programs.

If you are aware of private counselors or social service agencies that are working well with families, ask these people/groups to participate in your programs.

Enrichment programs can be offered to parents whose children attend one or more schools, or programs can be geared toward the entire district. One may also consider opening the program up to the entire community. Those families who may seem in particular need should be contacted directly by the school social worker/counselor.

- *When the program is new, you will have to work hard to get the word out.* Try to layer your marketing by printing pamphlets or posting on social media and websites. Likewise, layer your efforts on the ground through footwork. Attend other events or meetings where the parents you wish to reach may be. Tack up posters in neighborhood businesses and community centers.
- *Make lots of phone calls. Personal invitations are always best.*
- *Be clear that there is an open invitation for parents to bring friends or neighbors. They may need a ride, an interpreter, or moral support.*
- *At evening programs, always offer babysitting services or a program for children.* Sometimes the school honors society, Rotary or EarlyAct clubs may find this a natural fit for their club's role.
- *Consider the fact that you may be dealing with single parents or that they may have limited resources.*
- Keep this in mind while discussing the concepts of how to help support a child from being overly aggressive or passive and how to productively address conflict. This, in turn, becomes a natural avenue to address the concepts of harassment, intimidation, and bullying by parents, by modeling good conflict resolution skills.
- *Consider guest speakers.* Professionals in the community are usually happy to discuss topics that you select. It is a win-win situation—your program benefits from their expertise and they meet prospective clients.
- *Start with what you know, but then ask for input.* Initially, parenting programs can be conducted using an existing parenting education curriculum. As soon as possible, distribute surveys to parents, teachers, and administrators to identify other topics of interest that can be explored.
- *Include a parenting support component.* Parenting is a demanding job and sometimes it helps to hear that other parents face the same challenges. Be sure to allow some time for informal discussion among parents. Not only will they be able to voice their concerns and discuss their feelings, but they may also learn about strategies that have worked for others. If you listen carefully, you may just pick up some ideas for topics for future meetings.

THE DEVIL IS IN THE DETAILS

Some of the interventions and techniques you will see here may seem minor. Indeed, in the communicating of challenging conversations it is the minor and picayune that are the major issues. Think about your close relationships. It is often the little things your spouse or significant other does or does not do that create the biggest issues due to their recurrent cycles.

USE OF THE "I" MESSAGE

When one uses the word "you" (as in "I need to tell you what you did wrong"), it is an immediate knee-jerk reaction for the other party to become defensive. It is as if you are verbally pointing a finger to which the other party accordingly responds defensively and emotionally. Rather, using "I" as the first word in your statement takes that from an attack to a less personal perspective. Use of the words "I feel" is stated then as an opinion and, again, is less threatening to parents.

EMOTIONAL MIRRORS

The more emotion you put into a demanding conversation the greater the chance that the other party will mirror back the same emotion. Anger will be met with anger, agitated body language will be met with agitated body language, and so on. If you can't control the emotion or the anger, wait on the conversation if possible. If not, you risk an angry, unproductive conflict. Likewise, if a parent comes to you and is emotional remember emotion is not logical so don't try to legitimize emotion with logic.

Avoid body language such as crossing your arms, looking away for extended periods, looking at your watch, nervously tapping, or yawning. Remember that you can offend parents or put them off more by what you do than what you say.

THE CONVERSATION LIKELY DID NOT BEGIN WITH YOU ... BUT WILL LIKELY END WITH YOU

Most likely, the negative conversation that you are about to have did not start with you. The conversation was either due to a perceived pattern of transgressions that may have occurred at the teacher-parent, parent-parent, or student-parent level. This means that this issue may have festered for a while and it is now like playing a game of "telephone" in which the message has become unclear and intensified by either emotion or miscommunication.

Additionally, the problem may have been allowed to build up and fester over time and has now come to a head, which is brought to your attention in a fury of long-bottled emotions about a particular parental concern.

That being said then, it is critical to know where the issue began going off tracks and when the concern developed into something significant. This means first asking for a clarification of the history of the concern before delving into any aspect of the issue. It also means clearing the air about misconceptions, misquotes, and how issues may have been perceived to be handled in the past.

Remember being "right" does not solve a problem with parents. Proving you are "right" only serves to show that you are exerting power over them and has them leave with hard feelings. Finding a mutually acceptable solution shows the greatest level of respect among all parties.

Most importantly, it means, however, to get a good history of how you got to where you are with the issue at hand. It means listening closely to pinpoint opportunities for change as opposed to looking for the history as an "I got-cha" to prove the parents, or their facts and beliefs about how the problem got to where it is now, wrong.

WHAT IS IN A NAME? ... EVERYTHING

Be certain whenever possible to address parents by name. Why? Because it gives them the feeling that they are not just another nameless number in the batch of students that are under your care. Simply adding their name during your conflict with them will be a simple and subtle means of joining with them in a positive fashion. Often this is such an obvious courtesy we forget in the rush to handle the issue at hand.

REFLECTIVE LISTENING

One of the rarest commodities in a conversation is a good listener. How many times have you talked to a peer, spouse, or your children only to have them ask, "What did you say?" This is often a source of great frustration for all of us. So when you are meeting with parents be certain to provide them as much of you as possible.

Avoid distractions such as your phone or computer. Don't fiddle with objects, just try to devote as close to 100% of you as you can. It may sound simple, but when you have fifty things you have to do in a day, you may spend hours giving 50% of your ear to 100% of the people versus 100% of your ear to 50% of the people that need it most. Be present and give the present of your presence to those that need it most.

Strive for quality over quantity of conversation. If you are listening well to parents, you may not have to delve into an hour-long meeting only to find you are back where you started. Rather, you can listen and collaboratively come up with a quicker and often better solution. One of the best strategies for this is reflective listening:

- *Listen to what is being said.* Avoid interruptions and wait until a natural lull in the conversation takes place before saying anything.
- *Nod and makes statements such as "I see," "Uh huh, okay," to indicate that you understand each part of the statement being made to you.*
- *When you have a question, ask it.* Make sure it is truly a question to clarify and understand the viewpoint versus a sarcastic comment or a statement couched in the camouflage of a question.
- *Questions should clarify what you are interpreting with such statements as "so what you are telling me ...," "so the issue is ...," "help me to understand. ..."* In doing so, you are reflecting a real and genuine determination to comprehend what is going on.
- *Allow time for parents to correct your tentative understanding of what is being said.* It is okay that both parties disagree as long as it is for the sake of clarity for you to attempt to understand their viewpoint. Such phrases begin with comments such as, "No, what I am trying to tell you is. ...."
- *Be genuine in your interest.* A defining characteristic of a great leader it an ability to make a person feel listened to as if he or she is the only and most interesting person in the world. Really try to display an attentiveness to what the parent is saying.
- *Be Present:* When you are thinking of your next response, you are not listening. Pause and give the person time to talk without interruption.

TAKING CARE OF YOURSELF

It goes without saying that if you are not at 100% physically, your ability to deal with difficult parenting issues will not be at 100%. Additionally, your immunity to the stress, conflict, and discord are diminished reciprocally to the lack of appropriate self-care. Some of these may seem like common sense, however, they are worth stating.

- *Eat and sleep right.*
- *Avoid drinking and drugs.*
- *Exercise (according to the limits set by your medical professional).*
- *Know your limits. Say no to the things you need to say no to because you can only spread the 100% of yourself so thin.*
- *Set time away from the job. If you don't set a schedule, your schedule will set you. Set limits to work life and do not equate working longer with working more efficiently.*

- *Develop hobbies outside of school.*
- *Schedule quality time with family and friends. If you do not, these items will likely be the first two off your agenda.*

NOTES

* "Developmental Psychology." Wikipdedia Foundation, n.d. Web 19 May 2016.

    1. Covey, Stephen R. *The Seven Habits of Highly Effective People.* Place of Publication Not Identified.

Chapter 8

The Elephant in the School

Expanding Your Conflict Skills to Other Members of the School Community

When there's an elephant in the room, you can't pretend it is not there and just discuss the ants.

—Ellen Wittlinger*

EXTENDING YOUR SKILLS TO FACULTY

The skills of conflict resolution that you utilize with parents' parallel nicely with the skills you can use with fellow peers, faculty members, and coworkers. In this next chapter we will focus on how the abilities you developed for handling parents can be carried over as great skills for addressing faculty.

Again, we all go through life with our own ways of handling relationships. Each of us has our strengths and comfortable means of relating with the world both at home and vocationally. Do not think of any of the types as negative or overly positive; rather, think of these as ways you as well as your faculty members and fellow peers relate with the world that is around them. Avoid seeing these as manipulative or negative but as, like a personality type, part of a person that has both flipsides of strengths and weaknesses in each of the particular paradigms.

TYPES OF CHALLENGING FACULTY MEMBERS AND HOW TO DEAL WITH THEM

We all know these faculty members. As we go through these types, I am sure names and faces will flash in front of you. Each of these staff personalities requires unique tools and interventions with which to address them when

93

confronted with a tough conversation. Your tool belt requires that you have multiple specialized tools for each of these persons. Flexibility in stretching your comfort level to extend to these types is vital in navigating the school terrain.

An Ear to the Ground

As approachable and open as an educational leader you think you are, you will be generally insulated from the bubbling up of potential negative crises. Why? Leslie Gaines-Ross, chief reputation strategist at public relations firm Weber Shandwick, states in a study of CEOs and their length of career, "It's easy to get a bit insulated at the top, so you have to pursue honest feedback, even to the point of being uncomfortable."

It is natural for this insulation to be created by faculty. Who wants to be the messenger to convey the bad news to the boss? You know what they do to the messenger? Therefore, be certain that you find those faculty members who will be honest with you. Seek out those who have discerning views from your own and who will periodically check in and tell you what you don't want to hear when you most need to hear it. This will help prevent seemingly minor issues from becoming wildfires.

LISTEN FIRST AND REFLECT

When you must approach a faculty member about a difficult issue or vice versa, listen to his or her viewpoint first. This will usually give you some point of agreement or, at the very least, a better opportunity to figure out his or her. Avoid talking or expressing your opinion initially—listen, listen, listen.

Silence is sometimes appropriate after a difficult discussion to let the gravity of what was discussed "sink in." At times, we may be uncomfortable by the silence but avoid filling the vacuum with useless chatter or empty statements. Is your comment going to have any value to the current challenging conversational dialogue?

DON'T BE RUSHED TO JUDGMENT

Rarely are there matters of life and death in leadership and if everything is a crisis then nothing becomes a crisis because you have no priorities. If you are not in a position to deal with an issue, let the staff member know you need some time to think. Don't be rushed to judgment and then later regret what you said or change your mind and gain a reputation for being an inconsistent or a vacillating leader who is viewed as having ever-shifting values and a lack of vision, bouncing about as emotions strike you.

TYPES OF CHALLENGING FACULTY

"Leadership is not wielding authority—It's empowering people."

—Becky Brodin

The "Know It All" Faculty Member

These kinds of faculty members "know it all." Tell them something—too late; they already know of it. Teach them something—they have already been there, done it. These personnel are frustrating because although they teach, they appear to others as incapable of wanting to learn.

The following are interventions to attempt:

- *Recognize the insecurity as the heart of the matterV.* To admit not knowing is equated to being totally incompetent. Always balance assuring capabilities with behaviorally specific suggestions.
- *Plant the seed for change and see if they implement your suggestion into action.* Remember that it is the nature of these staff members to immediately react with "know that, done that." However, just because they say that and seem to deny your advice doesn't mean they won't react to your suggestion.
- *Use internal professional development.* Have them witness a faculty member that is strong in the skill you want them to learn. If possible, allow them to similarly teach a skill that is their strength. Question each about what they have mutually learned. Remember your goal is not to have them admit that they learned something; it is to implement what they know.

The Passive-Aggressive Faculty Member

These can be the most difficult and insidious of faculty members. As the name suggests, they may seem innocuous and passive in their personality. That being said, however, behind the scenes, they are wreaking havoc and act seemingly innocent when confronted. They will forget things, procrastinate, and appear to indicate you are overreacting when you address an issue—all in an attempt to conceal their anger in a façade of indirect communications.

- *These faculty members will swear that they are not angry and their actions are not purposeful.* It is important if you see these patterns within these personality types, and that you are direct in your communication and statements.
- *Set limits:* These personnel do not tend to understand limits and boundaries. These have to be established early and clearly in black and white.

- *Be behaviorally specific:* Be specific with these staff members. They need to know and be told exactly what you expect and the consequences of not doing so, accordingly.
- *Be cautious:* If you are being "buttered up" with kind and over-the-top compliments that have no validation be wary that the polar opposite may be being said behind your back.

The Rumor Spreader

These staff members can be found in every school in the nation. They are lurking in faculty rooms, trolling social media, and questioning everyone about the latest rumor, so that they can be the first to dish it to the masses yearning to hear the latest gossip about the goings on of the school. Then, like a dutiful gardener, they spread the seeds of rumor and innuendo carefully among the faculty of the building.

- *Be an open book.* Telling your staff what you can in an honest and open fashion eliminates the steam and zeal from some of the rumormonger's arsenal.
- *Encourage your staff to come to you, not go to their coworkers, with questions or to clarify inaccuracies.*
- *Address the faculty members directly with clear, accurate, and appropriate information that they will then disseminate.*
- *Do not enter the realm of feeding or discussing potential rumors as this just gives the rumormonger more fuel to give credence to the gossip.*
- *Take advantage of the rumormonger's natural penchant to spread rumors:* Convey good news to the rumormonger. Good news, like bad, can be spread around and helps build your creditability as a positive leader.

The Impaired Educator

Education and life are stressful. When the two collide and a person does not have the means to handle the situation, he or she may turn to alcohol or drugs as an escape. This creates a liability and danger for all involved.

- *This issue needs to be dealt with immediately.* Some may believe that all it needs is some time and monitoring for continued progression; however, this only increases the chance of something tragic happening. If the impairment is being brought to the realm of work, it is too late for a simple verbal warning.
- *Don't procrastinate; this is an issue that cannot wait.*
- *Be certain to understand that the Health Insurance Portability and Accountability Act (HIPPA) and confidentiality laws extend to this issue well beyond board policy and procedure, so be certain to consult with the human resources (HR) director.*

- *A union representative, an HR representative, and a counselor should be present when intervening.*
- *Document, document, document! Ensure that your documentation is of a factual and nonjudgmental nature.*

The "Star" Employee

This is the educator that you hope they consider cloning when the technology becomes available. If you had a staff full of these people your job would be perfect. They are self-starters, hard workers, natural leaders, and are creative. Never do they utter a word of complaint; they just do what they should do proactively and go above and beyond their duties.

- *Avoid overburdening them.* In the field of education there is a tendency to give the best teachers the most challenging students because "they can handle them." Or worse yet, give them less desired roles because they "won't complain." We do not want to take advantage of their abilities.
- *Constant praise.* One of the leading issues as to why people leave an occupation is the lack of recognition. Whenever possible, a quick note on their desk or specific, verbal praise and recognition will help raise their spirits. Just because they don't complain or engage in conflict does not mean they are not in pain.
- *Flexibility begets flexibility:* These staff members are often flexible to a fault. Providing them the same courtesy will only gain more of the same. Remember, most people work to live and don't live to work.

The "Underperforming" Employee

The polar opposite of the "star" Employee, this staff member is mediocre at best and completely ineffective at worst. It is important to remember, however, that there are any number of reasons for poor performance.

- *Look toward past performance and ask open-ended questions if you see a sudden change in performance.*
- *Seek to understand what could be going on in this person's life that may affect his or her work.* This does not mean that you have to be intrusive, but if you comprehend what is going on you can seek an avenue to fix it.
- *Give the person every tool possible.* Internal professional development in the areas of weakness may provide tools, ideas, and perhaps secure lasting mentors to help with understanding the inner dynamics of the school environment.
- *Do not let this issue fester.* If this person is ineffective, as he or she continues through the year it is likely this employee will slip further into this

pattern. This becomes especially problematic if he or she is getting close to tenure.

The "Change Fearer"

These types are anxiety-ridden. They will complain and worry about any change that comes their way (real or imagined). Whether it be technology programs, a new curriculum, or a new student in their class, they become worried and may complain or fall apart emotionally when rattled with a new change to their fragile system of alteration.

To address these faculty members in a challenging conversation, think of the following:

- *Assure them that they are going to be okay.* These faculty members exhibit a lot of worry that they are going to not be able to juggle this new task or student on an already full plate. Work though the "what ifs" with them proactively.
- *Listen. This issue can't usually be fixed.* Now that education has become ever changing and frenetic, you are forced to always reinvent yourself as an educator. Be certain to listen to their concerns.
- *Wait.* These faculty members' initial response is anxiety. When the initial anticipatory fear subsides, these educators tend to actually handle new changes very well.
- *Educate.* With new programs, new education should go hand in hand. This may seem obvious but it is not always the case. Many times new curricula or new programs are thrust upon faculty with little or no training. This will cause these teachers to melt with worry and panic. Providing adequate professional training that encourages even the most basic of questions will help eliminate this anxiety and panic. Professional development, however, must be internal to the school and engaging for these faculty members to fully envelop new curricula.

The "Martyr" Faculty Member

Just as there are bullies and targets in the student educational setting, so does this same dynamic play out in the larger adult work world. These kinds of employees always feel they are being victimized. They indicate victimization by the students, the parents, and (most strongly) the leadership they are typically under.

When you approach martyrs, they will feel sorry for themselves and say that you are not giving constructive feedback. Rather, they will take any suggestion as a direct attack on their very being and see you, or anyone else who criticizes them, as a bully who is going after them.

The following are ways to carefully enter the realm of a conversation with these staff members:

- *Focus on results not the person:* These faculty members tend to find conversations that are challenging in nature as an attack against their very being, and become emotional. With them, focus clearly on outcome-based measures. That is, what they are (or are not) producing during the school day. Avoid falling into the emotional pitfalls of feeling sorry for them, which will distract from the larger issue of responsibility.
- *Offer them productive criticism:* Focus on the details of what you want them to do. These staff members tend to look toward the negative and what they are perceived to be doing wrong. This is not useful for anyone. Instead, focus on the "what they can do" and be as detailed as need be.
- *Start off with honey and not the vinegar:* Be certain to give these faculty members genuine positive feedback. It is important to be cautious as they have a very perceptive antenna for BS; so if you cannot sincerely begin with positive feedback, avoid it.

The "Bully" Faculty Member

The "bully" faculty member is the polar opposite of the "martyr." This employee is similar to the parent of the same category (mentioned earlier).

These individuals will tend to push boundaries eternally and push others verbally and emotionally to get their way. They will use this strategy because it works for them to some degree. The mission statement of these faculty members are, "If I want something I will get it and those who are in the way are objects to be pushed out of the way or run over." Just like schoolyard bullies, they will also engage in name calling and teasing people. The difference now is they couch their behavior in terms of "just kidding" with others despite the fact that their humor is biting toward others.

- *These faculty members are typically the ones who will get into trouble for harassment.* The very nature of these employees and their often narcissistic ways lead to harassing others or having little understanding of concern for feelings. These employees need to be made aware of the legal definition of harassment and you may involve human resources as well to address disciplinary issues.
- *Make sure you set up strong boundaries with these staff.* These faculty members tend to think about themselves and what they need to do to accomplish what they want. They will be team players only when they have something to gain. Likewise, they will abandon the team the minute they get what they want or something better comes along. Without strong

boundaries they will go rogue to get only what they want. They will climb the ladder while stepping on the heads of others only for the boost to get to the top.

- *Address the behavior immediately.* These faculty members are always testing boundaries. If you do no teach them early, they see you as weak. If you are weak, you are another victim to be rolled over or pushed out of the way.

The "Butt Kisser" Faculty Member

These are the faculty members who always try to butter you up or cozy up to you and will do anything to get in your good graces. This can be flattering at first—someone who wants to do everything you ask; someone who is at your beck and call. Be cautious, however, the "butt kissers" always have an alternate agenda. Whether it be to gain advancement in some way or to insulate themselves for getting in trouble for a later indiscretion, there is always a purpose for their behavior aside from "just trying to be nice."

- *Avoid favoritism:* It is a natural inclination to want to place someone who is seemingly going out of their way for you on a pedestal. Be careful, as faculty members see this and it can lead to challenging conversations later with other staff.
- *Don't accept gifts:* As with the "passive-aggressive" parents, their gifts are a slippery slope. From their perspective, if you accept gifts, it is actually an acknowledgment that you are in collusion with them. It is a token that you are now friends and you will not have a challenging conversation with them. Boundaries are blurred and so are hierarchies and chains of command.
- *Reward them for their behaviors that pertain to work.* Conversations should be restricted to appreciating them when they do a sincerely good job within their job responsibilities. Avoid giving them praise when they are trying to schmooze with you as this will only serve to reinforce undesired behavior.
- *Don't Mix Business and Pleasure:* Try to avoid seeing these staff members out of school in a social environment, as they often do not understand the distinction between social and professional boundaries. Avoid this if possible.

The "Brand New" Teacher

A new teacher will generally not allow you to get close enough for a difficult conversation if they can help it. Many try to fly under the radar for fear that a difficult conversation will occur. Their worry over a lack of tenure puts them in a precarious position and so they should do nothing to rock the boat with any supervisor.

Here are some considerations when dealing with these delicate new staff members in tough conversations:

- *Do not procrastinate in these conversations.* Address them immediately so they can correct the issue before behaviors and habits become more deeply engrained.
- *Be very behaviorally specific.* If you are going to address a new teacher's style be specific with what you want him or her to do versus what he or she should cease doing.
- *Help them understand that criticism is a part of the learning process*: Often when you offer help or advice it is taken as a concern that you believe they are not good teachers. It is vital that new teachers understand that watching others and looking for ideas from seasoned teachers, as well as making mistakes, are all part of the growing process.
- *Encourage openness:* Some of the less experienced teachers will close their doors and try to teach without asking for any help. They will try their best to not seek out assistance because, again, this is seen as a sign of weakness and lack of independence. Actively encouraging their seeking out veteran teachers in learning groups—in a proactive fashion— will go a long way in avoiding uncomfortable dialogues.

The "Debbie Downer" Faculty Member

These members are sprinkled among any faculty body. They are the staff members who perpetually find the glass half empty. In fact, they seem to find everyone's glasses half empty, in the middle of the desert with a major water shortage. These faculty members get under your nerves because they will always point out the negative and drain the energy of yourself and the team.

- Allow them a finite amount of time to meet with you: They can drain your energy in a conversation and, unfortunately, sometimes have nothing to add that will be of benefit to you, your faculty, or them. If you extend your conversation with this faculty member it will become an ever-swirling whirlpool of negativity.
- Ask them to offer solutions versus problems. These faculty members are masters at finding problems. This is the easy part of a conversation; playing armchair quarterback and telling you what is wrong will not help anyone involved. Forcing them into a problem-solving versus problem-seeking paradigm changes the momentum of the conversation toward solution-focused aspects.
- Do not take what they say or do or what others say they do personally: There is a very real concern that these faculty members will be damaging

to the staff and that you need to head them off at the pass to avoid their negative nature become a contagion among other staff members.

• The truth is, the staff will quickly pick up this attribute and insulate themselves from these faculty members. At first, they will examine their environment to determine whether it is truly as perilous and negative as these "Debbie downers" state. Once they realize that it is not (and the sky is not falling in), the other staff members will immediately become tuned out. One caveat: should the school climate deteriorate, these are the first people who will ring the bell of concern and should be the first ones you meet with to avoid further decline of the work environment.

The "Lack of Boundaries" Faculty Member

These faculty members are guilty of "TMI"—too much information. They share with you, and everyone else, too much all the time. They are an open book and they never know when to shut that book or only give access to certain chapters. They will convey to students, other faculty members, and parents information that borders on the unprofessional and, as a result, blur the roles between comfort and unprofessionalism. This can make others uncomfortable, on one end, and on the other side of the spectrum can be considered as harassment or stepping over the line. Many times these faculty members simply don't understand where boundaries between the many persons they interact with during the day begin and end.

When dealing with these persons:

• *Be certain to model appropriate boundaries.* It is easy to get caught up in the blurred boundaries and to mistake their open nature for mere friendliness.
• *Educate and watch for issues of possible perceived harassment.* Remember, these people have difficulties with limits and may not realize when they step over the line and violate someone else's sensitivities.

Let them know directly when what they perceive as lighthearted humor or joking is not appropriate in nature and is "over the top."

The "Drama King/Queen" Faculty Member

These faculty members are somewhat similar to the "martyr" faculty members in that they have a lot of emotion. These faculty members, however, are always ready to ring the bell that the proverbial sky is falling down in your school. To them, everything is an emergency, they over exaggerate everything, and drain a lot of energy from their empathetic peers.

In dealing with these faculty members, remember:

- Be calm and relaxed: if they feel you are worried (they have an extremely good sense for this) they will feed off of this and worry more.
- Be clear and direct in your instruction: If they get direction of what to expect this will help them from worrying too much.
- Don't convey half information to them: If you don't know all the information on something, or it is only tentative, don't tell them. If you provide them only a little snippet of what you know, they panic believing that you are hiding something from them and become fearful.
- Faculty will become tired: When other faculty members begin to realize the extent of their drama, some may join in. Most will shy away as they drain too much energy to deal with on a consistent basis.

NOTE

* "Ellen Wittlinger." Ellen Wittlinger. N.p., n.d. Web. 16 July 2016.

Afterword

Education is learning what you didn't even know you didn't know.

—Daniel J. Boorstin*

Having a challenging conversation with a family is never an easy prospect. One takes a great deal of risk as you bring up what is the most potentially volatile subject: their child and his or her future.

All of us as parents strive to give our children the brightest future possible. We seek a hope for a far brighter tomorrow for our next generation than we had for our own. We want to protect them from bullying, sadness, and others that seek to discourage or put obstacles in the way of their aspirations, hopes, and dreams.

When educators say that they have to talk about a child's education it is never a simple conversation. The interaction employs so much more behind the scenes than we may appreciate or realize. We are generally talking about deeply emotional and heart-wrenching issues than meet the eye. In order for us to understand why parents become oppositional, sensitive, or even outright angry, we must step back and understand the larger picture.

As educators and educational leaders our job becomes ever more complicated. Curriculum and standardized testing are constantly changing at an evermore frenetic pace. Yet one thing never changes: the importance of the relationships with our students and our parents. It has not changed and will not change. Despite all the technology and gimmicks that seem to replace communication, nothing can replace a listening ear, a kind word, or the guidance that you as educators provide to those you work with each and every day.

Thank you for taking the opportunity to read this book. As an educator you did not go into the field for money, but to make a difference. I wish you the very best of luck as you continue to work hand in hand with the parents to sculpt our next generation of citizens to be even better than what we have inherited. I give you my heartfelt thanks again for taking time out of your full schedule to listen, and I wish you the best in using what you have learned.

NOTE

* "Daniel J. Boorstin Quote." Brainy Quote. Xplore, n.d. Wed. 20 July 2016.

Assertiveness Self-Assessment

Where Do You Fall on the Assertiveness Spectrum?

First, write down numbers from 1 to 10 on a piece of paper. Second, depending on your choice in each question, write a, b, or c after each number. Third, after answering all of the questions, refer to the SCORE INTERPRETATION KEY at the bottom of this page.

1. You are in a restaurant and order a steak medium-rare, but it is served to you well done. You would:
    a. Accept it since you sort of like it well done anyway.
    b. Angrily refuse the steak and insist on seeing the manager to complain about the poor service.
    c. Call the waiter and indicate you ordered your steak medium-rare, then turn it back.
2. You are a customer waiting in line to be served. Suddenly, someone steps in line ahead of you. You would:
    a. Let the person be ahead of you since he/she is already in line.
    b. Pull the person out of line and make him/her go to the back.
    c. Indicate to the person that you are in line and point out where it begins.
3. After walking out of a store where you purchased some items you discover you were shortchanged. You would:
    a. Let it go since you are already out of the store and have no proof you were shortchanged.
    b. Go to the manager and indicate how you were cheated by the clerk, then demand the proper change.
    c. Return to the clerk and inform him/her of the error.

4. You are in the middle of watching a very interesting television program when your spouse comes in and asks you for a favor. You would:
   a. Do the favor as quickly as possible, then return to the program to finish watching it.
   b. Say "no," then finish watching your program.
   c. Ask if it can wait until the program is over and, if so, do it then.

5. A friend drops in to say hello, but stays too long, preventing you from finishing an important work project. You would:
   a. Let the person stay, then finish your work another time.
   b. Tell the person to stop bothering you and to get out.
   c. Explain your need to finish your work and request he/she visit another time.

6. You ask a gas station attendant for five dollars' worth of gas. However, he fills up your tank by mistake and asks for twelve dollars. You would:
   a. Pay the twelve dollars since the gas is already in your tank and you will eventually need it anyway.
   b. Demand to see the manager and protest being ripped off.
   c. Indicate you only requested five dollars' worth of gas and give him only five dollars.

7. You suspect someone of harboring a grudge against you, but you don't know why. You would:
   a. Pretend you are unaware of his/her anger and ignore it, hoping it will correct itself.
   b. Get even with the person somehow so he/she will learn not to hold grudges against you.
   c. Ask the person if they are angry, then try to be understanding.

8. You bring your car to a garage for repairs and receive a written estimate. But later, when you pick up your car, you are billed for additional work and for an amount higher than the estimate. You would:
   a. Pay the bill since the car must have needed the extra repairs anyway.
   b. Refuse to pay, and then complain to the Motor Vehicle Department or the Better Business Bureau.
   c. Indicate to the manager that you agreed only to the estimated amount, then pay only that amount.

9. You invite a good friend to your house for a dinner party, but your friend never arrives and neither calls to cancel nor to apologize. You would:
   a. Ignore it, but manage not to show up the next time your friend invites you to a party.
   b. Never speak to this person again and end the friendship.
   c. Call your friend to find out what happened.

10. You are in a group discussion at work that includes your boss. A coworker asks you a question about your work, but you don't know the answer. You would:
    a. Give your coworker a false, but plausible answer so your boss will think you are on top of things.
    b. Do not answer, but attack your coworker by asking a question you know he/she could not answer.
    c. Indicate to your coworker you are unsure just now, but offer to give him/her the information later.

SCORE INTERPRETATION KEY

In general, there are three broad styles of interpersonal behavior. These are: a) Passive, b) Aggressive, and c) Assertive.

a. The Passive style of interpersonal behavior is characterized by inaction. People utilizing this style tend to be easy to get along with and pleasant, but unwilling to stand up for their rights, for fear of offending others. They are very uncomfortable expressing anger and usually deny or suppress this feeling should it occur. As a result, resentment can easily build under the surface producing stress and tension. In time, these people learn to fear close relationships because they have no way to protect themselves from the petty annoyances and inadvertent intrusions that occur in most relationships.

   The "a" choices in the quiz are representative of the Passive style. Thus, the more "a" choices you made, the more passive you are. Six or more "a" choices suggest you are probably passive in your interpersonal behavior.

b. The Aggressive style is characterized by intrusiveness. People who utilize this style tend to go after what they want, but are unconcerned about how this will affect others. Their angry, dominating manner tends to alienate people who, in time, may seek to oppose them. Aggressive individuals are usually suspicious of others and are often on the lookout for infractions or violations of their rights. Thus, the Aggressive style produces stress and prohibits the development of close, trusting, and caring interpersonal relationships.

   The "b" choices in the quiz are representative of the Aggressive style. Thus, the more "b" choices you made, the more aggressive you are. Six or more "b" choices indicate you are most likely aggressive in your interpersonal behavior.

c. The Assertive style is characterized by both fairness and strength. Assertive individuals are able to stand up for their rights, but remain sensitive to the rights of others. People who choose this style are usually relaxed and easy going, but are honest about their feelings. This is the best style for minimizing stress and maintaining long-standing intimate relationships.

The "c" choices in the quiz are representative of the Assertive style. Thus, the more "c" choices you made, the more assertive you are. Six or more "c" choices suggest you are probably assertive.

Look at the "c" answers again. If you move your everyday behavior closer to the "c" style of response, you will likely experience an increase in feelings of self-esteem and a decrease in feelings of stress.

There are always exceptions, however, as common sense would indicate. Some situations do call for more aggressive reactions and others are better handled using a more passive approach.

HOW SELF-ASSERTIVE ARE YOU? USED WITH PERMISSION, © 1990, Donald A. Cadogan, Ph.D.[1]

NOTE

1. "HOW SELF-ASSERTIVE ARE YOU?" Assertiveness Quiz. Accessed March, 2016. http://oaktreecounseling.com/assrtquz.htm.

Appendix B

Conflict Styles Survey

Below are statements that reflect various conflict strategies. As you read each statement, ask yourself honestly: *"How appropriate would this strategy be as a method for resolving conflict in my personality?"* Use the following scale to rate the desirability of each statement below.

1	*2*	*3*	*4*	*5*
completely undesirable	*undesirable*	*neither desirable nor undesirable*	*appropriate*	*very desirable*

____ 1. You scratch my back; I'll scratch yours.

____ 2. When two quarrel, he who keeps silent first is the most praiseworthy.

____ 3. Soft words win hard hearts.

____ 4. A person who will not flee will make his foe flee.

____ 5. Come and let us reason together.

____ 6. It is easier to refrain than to retreat from an argument.

____ 7. Half a loaf is better than none.

____ 8. A question must be answered by knowledge, not by numbers, if it's to have a right decision.

____ 9. When someone hits you with a stone, hit him with a piece of cotton.

___ 10. The arguments of the strongest always have the most weight.

___ 11. By digging and digging, the truth is discovered.

___ 12. Smooth words make smooth ways.

___ 13. If you cannot make a man think as you do, make him do as you do.

___ 14. He who fights and runs away lives to fight another day.

___ 15. A fair exchange brings no quarrel.

___ 16. Might overcomes right.

___ 17. "An eye for an eye" is fair play.

___ 18. Kind words are worth much and cost little.
___ 19. Seek 'til you find, and you'll not lose your labor.
___ 20. Kill your enemies with kindness.
___ 21. He loses least in a quarrel who keeps his tongue in cheek.
___ 22. Try, and trust will move mountains.
___ 23. Put your foot down where you mean to stand.
___ 24. One gift for another makes good friends.
___ 25. Don't stir up a hornet's nest.

Transfer your rating numbers to the blanks below.

The numbers correspond to the proverb numbers. Total each column.

5	4	1	2	3
8	10	7	6	12
11	13	15	9	18
19	16	17	14	20
22	23	24	21	25
Column 1	Column 2	Column 3	Column 4	Column 5

Each of the above columns contains statements that reflect the following conflict styles.

Column 1 = Win-Win Problem-Solving; Assertive
Column 2 = Forcing; Aggressive
Column 3 = Compromising
Column 4 = Withdrawing; Non-Assertive
Column 5 = Smoothing; Accommodating

Written permission granted by Cinnie Noble, CINERGY® Coaching, www.cinergycoaching.com[1]

NOTE

1. "CINERGY Coaching." *CINERGY Coaching*. Web. 02 March 2016.

Appendix C

Verbal Aggressiveness
Self-Assessment

This scale is designed to measure how people try to influence others. For each statement, indicate the extent to which you feel it is true for you in your attempts to influence others. Use the following scale:

1	2	3	4	5
almost never true	*rarely true*	*occasionally true*	*often true*	*almost always true*

_____ 1. I am extremely careful to avoid attacking individuals' intelligence when I attack their ideas.

_____ 2. When people are very stubborn, I use insults to soften the stubbornness.

_____ 3. I try very hard to avoid having other people feel bad when I try to influence them.

_____ 4. When people refuse to do a task I know is important, without good reason, I tell them they are unreasonable.

_____ 5. When others do things I regard as stupid, I try to be extremely kind and gentle with them.

_____ 6. If others I am trying to influence really deserve it, I attack their character.

_____ 7. When people behave in ways that are in very poor taste or inappropriate in nature, I insult them in order to shock them into proper behavior.

_____ 8. I try to make people feel good about themselves even when their ideas are stupid or dumb.

_____ 9. When people simply will not budge on a matter of importance, I lose my temper and say rather harsh things to them.

_____ 10. When people criticize my shortcomings, I take it in good humor and do not try to get back at them.

113

_____ 11. When individuals insult me, I get a lot of pleasure out of really telling them off.

_____ 12. When I dislike someone, I try not to show it in what I say or how I say it or offend them in any way.

_____ 13. I like making fun and teasing people who do things that are very stupid in order to make them think.

_____ 14. When I attack a person's ideas, I try not to damage their self-concept or personality.

_____ 15. When I try to influence another, I make a great effort not to offend them.

_____ 16. When people do things that are mean or cruel, I attack their character in order to help correct their behavior.

_____ 17. I refuse to participate in arguments when they involve personal attacks.

_____ 18. When nothing seems to work in trying to influence others, I yell and scream in order to get some movement from them.

_____ 19. When I am not able to refute someone's position, I try to make them feel defensive in order to weaken their position.

_____ 20. When an argument shifts to personal attacks, I try very hard to change the subject.

Transfer your rating numbers to the blanks below.

The numbers correspond to the statement numbers.

Step 1: *Add* your scores for items 2, 4, 6, 7, 9, 11, 13, 16, 18, 19.
Step 2: *Add* your scores on items 1, 3, 5, 8, 10, 12, 14, 15, 17, 20.
Step 3: *Subtract* the sum obtained in Step 2 from 60.
Step 4: *Add* total obtained in Step 1 to result obtained in Step 3. Compare to below.

2	1
4	3
6	5
7	8
9	10
11	12
13	14
16	15
18	17
19	20
_____	_____
Step 1	Step 2

SCORING

59–100: High level of verbal aggressiveness
39–58: Moderate level of verbal aggressiveness
20–38: Low level of verbal aggressiveness

Written permission granted by Cinnie Noble, CINERGY® Coaching, www.cinergycoaching.com[1]

NOTE

1. "CINERGY Coaching." *CINERGY Coaching*. Web. 02 March 2016.

Appendix D

Conflict Resilience Quotient (CQ)

Something that happens to many of us in the aftermath of interpersonal conflict is a tendency to agonize about what happened. We may criticize ourselves—wishing we had said something else or differently. We may blame the other person and not let go of our feelings about him or her. We may continue to ruminate about unresolved hurts and issues. We may make the situation bigger than it was, or try to minimize it while still experiencing a huge impact that we try to suppress.

The Conflict Resilience Quotient Inventory below will help you understand how well you handle conflict. Are you the kind of person who can address a conflictual situation and let it roll off your back and move on with your day? Or are you the kind of person that will let one issue with a parent or faculty member bring you down and leave you stuck on the issue for the day, emotionally spent and wondering if you should have ever entered the field?

On a scale of 1 (Less True) to 5 (Most True), after most interpersonal conflicts, I usually tend to:	
Recover quickly and do not worry, agonize or stay preoccupied about what the other person said or did that offended me.	1 2 3 4 5
Forgive and do not bear a grudge about the other person and what s/he said or did. Or if I am not ready to forgive yet, I don't let the interaction weigh me down.	1 2 3 4 5
Reflect on what I learned from the conflict that will help me manage future disagreements.	1 2 3 4 5
Reach out to make amends with the other person, or talk out and clarify our differences.	1 2 3 4 5

Take responsibility for my part of the conflict and consider what I may have done differently.	1 2 3 4 5
Not share my side of the situation with others in self-serving and distorted ways.	1 2 3 4 5
Feel hopeful that things will be better and consider how I will try to contribute positively to this happening.	1 2 3 4 5
Move on and not see myself as a victim or feel sorry for myself.	1 2 3 4 5
Not continue to perceive the other person in negative ways.	1 2 3 4 5
Not gossip about and bad-mouth the other person to others.	1 2 3 4 5
Identify what may have been important to the other person that I did not realize before.	1 2 3 4 5
Apologize for my part of the conflict.	1 2 3 4 5
Have a better appreciation for and understanding of the other person's perspective on the issues, even if I don't agree with it.	1 2 3 4 5
Let go of blaming the other person for what he/she did or said (or didn't say or do).	1 2 3 4 5
Not criticize, blame myself or engage in other self-deprecating behaviors about what I did or said (or didn't say or do).	1 2 3 4 5
Total	

SCORING KEY
15–39: You are very sensitive to conflict.
40–54: Your recovery from conflict is moderate. Use caution.
55–69: You are okay with conflict.
70–75: You have armor for conflict.

Written permission granted by Cinnie Noble, CINERGY® Coaching, www.cinergycoaching.com

Appendix E

Parenting Quiz

1. A neighbor comes to visit, but your five-year-old son hides behind you. You would:
   a. Scold him for being shy and make him say hello.
   b. Ignore his shyness and let him gradually overcome it as he gets older.
   c. Apologize for his shyness and explain that he is just little.
   d. Ignore his shyness, but show pleasure any time he interacts with your neighbor.
2. Your ten-year-old daughter comes to breakfast late and in her pajamas. It is now too late for her to dress, eat, and make it to school on time. You would:
   a. Scold her for being late and restrict her evening activities.
   b. Let her go to school late, and let her deal with her teacher herself.
   c. Dress her while she eats and get her to school on time.
   d. Give her a choice of either dressing at home and eating in the car, or eating at home and dressing in the car. But you let her decide.
3. Your son gets a D on his report card and feels discouraged. You would:
   a. Take away TV until he improves his grade.
   b. Say nothing since his other marks are good.
   c. Console him by fixing his favorite meal.
   d. Tell him that you know he feels sad, but he did well in his other subjects and you appreciate his efforts.
4. Your overweight daughter tells you boys never call her and she has no date for the school dance. You would:
   a. Tell her boys would probably call her if she wasn't overweight, then restrict her diet.
   b. Tell her not to worry because she will find another boy someday.

   c. Tell her no matter what others think you will always love her, and others will love her too.

   d. Empathize with her concerns, but remind her she may have to choose between being popular and satisfying her craving for sweets.

5. Your daughter tells you her little brother cheated her in a game. You would:

   a. Scold your son for cheating and temporarily remove one of his toys.

   b. Tell her not to get upset because he is only little.

   c. Play with her yourself for a while and tell her you are proud of her for not cheating.

   d. Tell her you know it is not fun to feel cheated, but you're confident she can work it out with her brother.

6. Your son tracks mud on your clean kitchen floor. You would:

   a. Scold him and make him clean it up.

   b. Ignore it because it was an accident.

   c. Clean it up for him since boys will be boys.

   d. Tell him you are annoyed, and he can either clean his muddy shoes when he comes in, or not wear them in the house. You then discuss cleaning the floor.

7. Your son promised to come home on time for dinner, but arrives an hour late. You would:

   a. Punish him by depriving him of dinner.

   b. Say nothing since he is now safely home.

   c. Tell him you were worried about him.

   d. Tell him how you feel when he doesn't keep his word, then let him eat the cold leftovers.

8. Your six-year-old daughter refuses to eat her dinner. You would:

   a. Insist she eat before letting her leave the table.

   b. Disregard it and let her skip dinner.

   c. Tell her how important it is for her to eat good food.

   d. Feed her something else nutritious that she likes.

9. Your nine-year-old son comes to the dinner table dirty. You would:

   a. Tell him he is filthy, and then make him wash.

   b. Let him eat that way since boys always get dirty.

   c. Get the wash cloth for him and help him wash.

   d. Remind him of the family rule that people who wish to eat here must be clean then remove his plate until he has washed.

10. Your twelve-year-old daughter refuses to set the table before dinner as she agreed. You would:

   a. Make her set the table then restrict her TV that night.

   b. Forget about it since no child is perfect, and remind yourself that she will set it when she has her own place.

   c. Set the table for her, but remind her how much you appreciate it when she does.

   d. Delay dinner until her chore is complete. If she still refuses, go out to dinner with your spouse.

ANSWERS

All good parenting is guided by strong feelings of love and respect for the children. How these feelings are translated into day-to-day parenting is variable according to the personalities of each parent. The interaction of parent personality and family love produces a kaleidoscope that is an individualized parental style. Most of our parenting falls within a few easily identifiable styles.

In general, there are four broad styles of parenting which we will label: a) Firm/Rigid, b) Relaxed/Passive, c) Nurturing/Protective, and d) Flexible/Democratic.

   a. FIRM/RIGID: The firm style is characterized by strong parental control and is often utilized by people who like to be in command. These parents expect their children to respect them and to do what they are told with little explanation, negotiation, or argument. The primary focus is on proper, respectful, or obedient behavior. The advantage of this mode, when successful, is that parents get well-behaved children, which is the source of pride in this parenting style. In addition, little in the way of talking back is expected. The children know firm and consistent rules for which there is little bend or negotiation.

      At the far end of this parenting style, can lead to parenting that is high in discipline while children don't feel they are given enough affection. In addition, the thoughts, feelings and conflict resolution skills of these children are stunted because they were only taught blind obedience. As a result, this parenting works only with younger children or with those who eventually lack the self-esteem to respond back in an assertive (or even aggressive) fashion.

      Nevertheless, the firm style, through its clarity and consistency, can instill feelings of security in children. However, when excessive, it does little to foster a mature, self-directed, and responsible attitude toward life. Instead, it tends to produce either rebelliousness or passive-conformity in children.

      The "a" responses in the quiz represent this method. Eight "a" choices indicate you may be a firm/rigid parent.

   b. RELAXED/PASSIVE: The relaxed style is characterized by an easygoing "laissez-faire" attitude toward the children. These parents understand

and provide room for their children's inert abilities to master their own problems and develop these at their own pace. In these families, children rarely are made to feel controlled, pressured, or guilty. With this ability to investigate and navigate the world around them, children develop a greater capacity for creative behavior. The primary strength of this style, at its optimum, is that these homes are low on stress, which allows family members an opportunity to foster feelings of warmth and comfort on a level that permeates all members of the family unit.

On the other side of the coin of this parenting style spectrum, however, these parents may demonstrate a high level of passivity and an "anything goes" attitude. In this exaggerated form of this parenting paradigm, they cross a line from simply being relaxed in their parenting style to being apathetic and letting everyone in the home do what they want. With families such as these, children cannot learn rules, boundaries, or the discipline needed for ultimate success in the world. Thus, excessively relaxed parents do little to teach their children responsible behavior and are poor role models for showing the full role of parenting. The payoff for these parents is that they do not put a lot into the parenting aspects and so have ample time to pursue their own ventures.

The "b" choices represent this mode. Eight "b" answers suggest you may be a relaxed/passive parent.

c. NURTURING/PROTECTIVE: The nurturing style of parenting is heavy on maternal nurturing. Children being fostered in this style are given as much love, affection, and warmth as possible and, reciprocally, this is most of what is expected in return. Children of these parents feel loved, cared for, and protected. Parents and children in these types of homes tend to be extremely close and caring toward one another. Due to the amount of caring heaped upon the child and little criticism, this style does the most toward building self-esteem in children.

In its extreme form, however, these parents are too involved with their children, do things for them to excess, and can be smothering (a.k.a. "the helicopter parent"). Their children are pampered and coddled, but learn little independent behavior. Excessively nurturing parents tend to be overly protective and seek perpetual appreciation from their children. Unfortunately, because they seldom do things on their own, their children tend to lack self-confidence or a sense of mastery. They often grow up feeling insecure and dependent as adults.

The "c" choices are indicative of this style. Eight or more "c" choices suggest you may be a nurturing/protective parent.

d. FLEXIBLE/DEMOCRATIC: The flexible style is usually seen in the families of happy children. This mode consists of a combination of the firm, relaxed, and nurturing styles utilized somewhat evenly and usually in a democratic fashion. The flexible style tends not to go to extremes in any mode. It is characterized by fairness, mutual respect, and openness to ideas from all family members. The natural consequences of one's behavior are usually stressed as the reason for making choices. Family rules are developed thorough discussion whenever possible. Although there are limits on what behavior is acceptable, and parents do have the ultimate say, nevertheless these parents do listen to their children and, within reason, try to meet their needs. Flexible parents endeavor to avoid strongly imposing their authority on their children. But when they do, because it is so infrequent, their children more readily comply.

The disadvantage of the flexible manner of parenting is that it takes time, patience, and the willingness to attend to childhood needs. Also, since the flexible parent has no single mode or guiding principle to follow, and since individual situations frequently differ, decisions about how to respond must often be made. This can produce feelings of uncertainty. However, since these parents are not stuck with any one style of response to family situations, they can react more rationally and be guided by the demands of the circumstance.

All this obviously takes more time. But in the long run time is usually saved, for the children from these families are generally better behaved and, thus, typically require less correction.

The "d" answers represent this style. Eight "d" responses suggest you are most likely a flexible/democratic parent.

It should also be noted, however, that the truly flexible parent would also choose answers in the "a," "b," or "c" groups. This is because the "d" choices are not the only effective or appropriate responses to the situations presented. Thus, a choice pattern that is somewhat evenly divided also indicates flexibility. And, of course, many other responses could easily be made and still foster a home atmosphere conducive to healthy emotional growth.

WHAT TYPE OF PARENT ARE YOU? USED WITH PERMISSION © 1990, Donald A. Cadogan, Ph.D.[1]**

NOTE

1. "WHAT TYPE OF PARENT ARE YOU?" Assertiveness Quiz. Accessed April, 2016. http://oaktreecounseling.com/assrtquz.htm.

Bibliography

Carr, Jelleff C. "Gallup Poll Rates Honesty and Ethical Standards." *Regulatory Toxicology and Pharmacology* 29, no. 1 (1999): 96. doi:10.1006/rtph.1998.1284.

"CINERGY Coaching." *CINERGY Coaching*. Web. 02 March 2016.

"CINERGY Coaching." *CINERGY Coaching*. Web. 02 March 2016.

Covey, Stephen R. *The Seven Habits of Highly Effective People*. Place of Publication Not Identified.

"Family Grief." *Counselling for Grief and Bereavement Counselling for Grief and Bereavement*, 55–79. doi:10.4135/9781446214800.n4.

Fisher, Roger, and William Ury. *Getting to Yes: Negotiating Agreement without Giving in*. New York, NY: Penguin, 2011, 99–108.

Gabor, Don. *How to Start a Conversation and Make Friends*. New York: Simon & Schuster, 2011.

Hanna, Laurie. "Delaware Parents Angry after School Accidentally Sends out 'Hurt Feelings Report' They Say Mocks Bullying." *New York Daily News* February, 19 2016. Web.

"How Blaming Teachers Shortchanges Students—NEA Today." NEA Today. 2012. Accessed February, 2016. http://neatoday.org/2012/11/26/how-blaming-teachers-shortchanges-students-2/.

"HOW SELF-ASSERTIVE ARE YOU?" Assertiveness Quiz. Accessed March, 2016. http://oaktreecounseling.com/assrtquz.htm.

Ito, Mamie. "Fundamental Attribution Schema." *PsycEXTRA Dataset*. doi:10.1037/e342482004-001.

Maslow, Abraham H., and Robert Frager. *Motivation and Personality*. New York: Harper and Row, 1987.

Mehrabian, Albert. *Silent Messages: Implicit Communication of Emotions and Attitudes*. Belmont, CA: Wadsworth Pub., 1981.

"N.J. Now Has More Than 100 School Religious Holidays You May Not Know About." Toms River, NJ Patch. 2016. Accessed April 12, 2016. http://patch.com/new-jersey/tomsriver/nj-approves-more-100-school-religious-holidays-you-may-not-know.

Novick, Brett "15 Ways to Involve 'At Risk' Parents" In Enrichment Programs, NJEA Review, December 2014.

Stone, Douglas, Bruce Patton, and Sheila Heen. *Difficult Conversations: How to Discuss What Matters Most.* New York, NY: Viking, 1999.

"Survey Finds Parent-teacher Relationships Strong—Teachers given Grade of." Rss. Accessed April 08, 2016. http://www.nea.org/home/51796.htm.

"The Teacher Dropout Crisis." NPR. Accessed April 08, 2016. http://www.npr.org/sections/ed/2014/07/18/332343240/the-teacher-dropout-crisis.

"Triangulation (family Dynamics)." Psychology Wiki. Accessed February, 2016. http://psychology.wikia.com/wiki/Triangulation_(family_dynamics).

"WHAT TYPE OF PARENT ARE YOU?" Assertiveness Quiz. Accessed April, 2016. http://oaktreecounseling.com/assrtquz.htm.

"Work to Implement the CCSS. The MetLife Survey of the ..." Accessed April 8, 2016. http://www.achieve.org/files/March2012Perspective.pdf.

Index

About the Author

Brett J. Novick holds a bachelor's degree in psychology from LaSalle University in Philadelphia, Pennsylvania, and a master's degree in family therapy from Friends University in Wichita, Kansas, as well as post-degree work and certification in school social work from Monmouth University in West Long Branch, New Jersey. Mr. Novick is licensed as a marriage and family therapist and state certified as a school social worker. He holds postgraduate certification as a supervisor, principal, and school administrator.

Mr. Novick has been working within school districts in New Jersey for the past fifteen years. In addition to his work as a school social worker/counselor, he has worked in private practice as well as a variety of community mental health settings with individuals, groups, and families. He also has experience working with children and families in crises as an in-home therapist. Mr. Novick supervised a therapeutic children's shelter for youth in the care and custody of the state of Missouri and was employed as a coordinator of a county program in that state for families that had a member with a developmental disability. He currently is an adjunct instructor at Rutgers University teaching postgraduate studies that deal with difficult parents, behavioral issues with students, practical social skills for classified students, personality disorders, special education issues, and parental enrichment.

He has written several national and international articles on education, educational administration, counseling, and social work. In addition, Mr. Novick was awarded District Teacher of the Year in 2007–2008 and New Jersey School Counselors Association Human Rights Advocate of the Year in 2008. Additionally, in 2011, he was honored with the NJ Council on Developmental

Disabilities Inclusive Educator of the Year Award & Fellowship. He has received the Ocean Personnel and Guidance Association (OCPGA) Ocean County Counselor of the Year, the Ocean County Human Services Advocate, the New Jersey Department of Education (NJDOE) Holocaust Education Commission's Hela Young Memorial Award as well as the New Jersey Education Association (NJEA) Dr. Martin Luther King Jr. Civil and Human Rights Award.